STUDY GUIDE

Following Jesus

The Gospel of Mark

W. Robert Godfrey

LIGONIER MINISTRIES
Renew your Mind.
LIGONIER.ORG | 800-435-4343

421 Ligonier Court, Sanford, FL 32771
E-mail: info@ligonier.org

Printed in China.

Contents

Introduction

The gospel of Mark lays out a vivid, swift, and dense narrative of Jesus' ministry. But often when we read the Gospels, we don't pick up on how they are organized and may think of them as stringing together one unconnected event after another. In this teaching series, Dr. W. Robert Godfrey takes a fresh look at the oldest gospel, giving keen insights into Mark's intent, structure, and message. As we follow Jesus through Mark's gospel, we catch a magnificent glimpse at His life, hearing the call to follow Him and, by God's Spirit, heeding the call to follow Him.

This study guide is a companion to the video teaching series. Whether you are using the DVDs, streaming the videos on Ligonier.org, or going through the course in Ligonier Connect, this resource is designed to help you make the most of the learning experience. For each message in the series, there is a corresponding lesson in this guide. Here is what you will find in each lesson:

INTRODUCTION	The introduction is a brief paragraph that summarizes the content covered in the lecture and considered in the study guide lesson. **How to use:** Use the introduction to each lesson to get a sense of the big picture before watching the video. Refer to these statements as you work through the study guide to remind yourself of what you have already covered and where you are headed.
LEARNING GOALS	The learning goals are the knowledge and skills that the study guide lesson will endeavor to equip you with as you work through the lecture content. **How to use:** Familiarize yourself with the goals of each lesson before engaging its contents. Keeping the overall purpose in mind as you watch each video and reflect on or discuss the questions will help you get the most out of each lesson.
KEY IDEAS	The key ideas are the major points or takeaways from the lecture. **How to use:** Use these ideas to prepare yourself for each lesson and to review previous lessons. They describe specifically the knowledge that each lecture is communicating.
REFLECTION & DISCUSSION QUESTIONS	The questions are the guided reflection and/or discussion component of the lesson that is intended to help you prepare for, process, and organize what you are learning. **How to use:** Reflect on individually or discuss in a group the questions in the order in which they appear in the lesson. The time stamps in the right margin indicate where the answers to questions during the video can be found.

PRAYER	The prayer section offers suggestions for how to close the lesson in prayer with respect to what was taught in the lecture. **How to use:** Consider using each lesson's prayer section as a guide to personal or group prayer. These sections follow the ACTS prayer model, which you can learn more about in R.C. Sproul's Crucial Questions booklet *Does Prayer Change Things?* This helpful guide is available as a free e-book at Ligonier.org.
REVIEW QUIZ	The review quiz is a set of six multiple-choice questions that appears at the end of each lesson. **How to use:** Use each quiz to check your comprehension and memory of the major points covered in each lecture. It will be most beneficial to your learning if you take a lesson's quiz either sometime between lessons or just before you begin the next lesson in the study guide.
ANSWER KEY	The answer key provides explanations for the reflection and discussion questions and answers to the multiple-choice questions in the review quiz. **How to use:** Use the answer key to check your own answers or when you do not know the answer. Note: Do not give in too quickly; struggling for a few moments to recall an answer reinforces it in your mind.

Study Schedules

The following table suggests four plans for working through the *Following Jesus* video teaching series and this companion study guide. Whether you are going through this series on your own or with a group, these schedules should help you plan your study path.

	Extended 28-Week Plan	Standard 26-Week Plan	Abbreviated 13-Week Plan	Intensive 9-Week Plan
Week	**Lesson**			
1	*	1	1 & 2	1–3
2	1	2	3 & 4	4–6
3	2	3	5 & 6	7–9
4	3	4	7 & 8	10–12
5	4	5	9 & 10	13–15
6	5	6	11 & 12	16–18
7	6	7	13 & 14	19–21
8	7	8	15 & 16	22–24
9	8	9	17 & 18	25–26
10	9	10	19 & 20	
11	10	11	21 & 22	
12	11	12	23 & 24	
13	12	13	25 & 26	
14	13	14		
15	14	15		
16	15	16		
17	16	17		
18	17	18		

	Extended 28-Week Plan	Standard 26-Week Plan	Abbreviated 13-Week Plan	Intensive 9-Week Plan
Week	**Lesson**			
19	18	19		
20	19	20		
21	20	21		
22	21	22		
23	22	23		
24	23	24		
25	24	25		
26	25	26		
27	26			
28	*			

* For these weeks, rather than completing lessons, spend your time discussing and praying about your learning goals for the study (the first week) and the most valuable takeaways from the study (the last week).

1

A Unique Gospel

INTRODUCTION

The gospel of Mark is the shortest of the four Gospels, but why did Mark write in such a spartan, fast-paced manner? What was his goal, and how does his style and structure reflect it? In this lesson, Dr. Godfrey gives an overview of Mark's gospel by explaining Mark's unique perspective on the life and ministry of Jesus.

LEARNING GOALS

When you have finished this lesson, you should be able to:

- Understand chiasms and their importance to the gospel of Mark
- Identify the distinctive aspects of Mark's writing style
- Know the goal and central point of Mark's gospel

KEY IDEAS

- Mark's gospel is built around a chiastic literary structure.
- The gospel of Mark is brief and abrupt but also vivid and thoughtful.
- Mark is chiefly about faith and the power of the gospel to save and encourage disciples of Christ.

REFLECTION & DISCUSSION QUESTIONS

Before the Video

What Do You Think?

Take a moment to answer the following questions. They will prepare you for the lecture.

- Why is it important to have the gospel written and not just passed down by word of mouth? How has having the written Word affected your life?

- What has stuck out to you about Mark's gospel in the past? How is it different from the other gospels?

Scripture Reading

These are written so that you may believe that Jesus is the Christ, the Son of God, and that by believing you may have life in his name.

—John 20:31

- What can the Word produce in those who hear it?

During the Video

Answer the following questions while you watch the video. They will guide you through the lecture.

Chiastic Structure *0:00–9:39*

- What is a chiasm? How does Dr. Godfrey explain chiasms?

- Why is the gospel of Mark so short? Why did Mark construct such a fast-paced narrative?

Style and Aim *9:39–24:14*

- What are some of the standout elements of Mark's writing?

- How does Mark challenge his readers to go beyond a simple, surface reading of the text?

- To whom is Mark writing? How does this goal shape the overall aim of the work?

After the Video

Answer the following questions after you have finished the lecture. They will help you identify and summarize the major points.

- How does Mark use chiasms to illustrate his main points? What do chiasms help show? What kind of information do they not show?

  If you are in a group, have the members reflect on ways that chapter and verse divisions can be both helpful and unhelpful. Ask: What are the benefits of a more natural approach to division, such as chiasms?

- What does it mean that Mark goes "beyond the simple immediate truth"? How do Mark's small details help fill in the larger message of his gospel?

  If you are in a group, have the members skim the gospel of Mark, using the chapter and section titles to guide them. Ask: What major themes do you see in the gospel?

- Why is the gospel not one of the "stories that trap us"? What does it do instead?

  If you are in a group, have the members give an example of how the gospel has liberated an aspect of their lives. Ask: How does God promise to liberate you from the stories of your past that attempted to trap you?

PRAYER

Commit what you have learned from God's Word in this lesson to prayer.

- Praise God for revealing Himself in Scripture and in His Son, Jesus Christ.
- Confess the ways that you may have taken familiar books of the Bible for granted.
- Thank God for preserving the good news of Jesus Christ in His Word so that you heard it and, by the working of His Spirit, believed.
- Ask God to continue sanctifying you by His Spirit through the truth of the gospel.

REVIEW QUIZ

Use these multiple-choice questions to measure what you learned from this lesson.

1. What frequent expression characterizes Mark's fast-paced writing style?
   a. Suddenly
   b. Immediately
   c. It came to pass
   d. Now
2. How does Mark use Isaiah in the opening of his gospel?
   a. He quotes Isaiah but inserts part of Malachi to contextualize it.
   b. He quotes Isaiah but inserts part of Haggai to prove that Jesus is the Lord.
   c. He quotes only Isaiah to prove that Jesus is the God of the Old Testament.
   d. He quotes only Isaiah but misquotes the referenced text.
3. How many sections does Dr. Godfrey divide Mark into?
   a. Eight
   b. Nine
   c. Eleven
   d. Sixteen
4. What are some examples of Mark's vivid style of writing?
   a. His description of Jesus' face as "shining like the sun" in the transfiguration
   b. The way that he describes the loaves as "large" in the feeding of the five thousand
   c. His addition of "wild animals" to Jesus' temptation in the wilderness
   d. Both a and c
5. The chapter divisions of the Bible are inspired by the Holy Spirit, but the verses are not.
   a. True
   b. False
6. What is the main virtue that Mark is looking to inspire in his audience?
   a. Love
   b. Hope
   c. Courage
   d. Faith

Answer Key—A Unique Gospel

REFLECTION & DISCUSSION QUESTIONS

Before the Video

What Do You Think?

These are personal questions. The answers should be based on your own knowledge and experience.

Scripture Reading

- What can the Word produce in those who hear it?

  God's Word is the primary means that the Holy Spirit uses to produce faith in His people because "faith comes from hearing, and hearing through the word of Christ" (Rom. 10:17), which is why John mentions that the purpose of his gospel is that readers might believe in Christ and have "life in his name" (John 20:31).

During the Video

Chiastic Structure

- What is a chiasm? How does Dr. Godfrey explain chiasms?

  Chiasms are an ancient literary device that organizes information in a way that helps readers to remember it. Dr. Godfrey compares it to an upside-down pyramid, in which each step up the pyramid corresponds to an opposite step down the pyramid, culminating in a single focal point that is the key part of the chiastic structure.

- Why is the gospel of Mark so short? Why did Mark construct such a fast-paced narrative?

  Mark's gospel is short because he wants to convey information in a "laser-like way," focusing only on what he wants to tell us about the life of Jesus. His narrative is very fast-paced to highlight the specific details of Christ's life with thoughtful intentionality.

Style and Aim

- What are some of the standout elements of Mark's writing?

  Mark's writing is extremely vivid, abrupt, and elusive. He gives many one-of-a-kind details in his gospel that help bolster the overall message that he is trying to convey. He also tends to abruptly start and stop his writing, so focused on essential details of the gospel that he rarely makes a full transition. Additionally, he is elusive by constantly hinting at and referencing things behind and beyond what's written.

- How does Mark challenge his readers to go beyond a simple, surface reading of the text?

  By alluding to other Scripture and further truths beyond the immediacy of his gospel, Mark makes many connections that force readers to dig deeper into his writing to find profound details that are not immediately apparent. He does this in the prologue where he quotes Isaiah, hinting that Isaiah's messianic prophecy is being fulfilled in Christ without stating it overtly.

- To whom is Mark writing? How does this goal shape the overall aim of the work?

  Mark is writing to people who already believe the gospel but may not know specific details of Jesus' life. Because this is his audience, he primarily writes to encourage these believers, strengthen their faith in Christ, and reveal more about Christ's message to them.

After the Video

- How does Mark use chiasms to illustrate his main points? What do chiasms help show? What kind of information do they not show?

  Mark uses chiasms to organize his information into compact but profound groupings and emphasize certain themes of his gospel. Chiasms work as a tool that prop up already existing themes in the text. They can highlight focal points or major redemptive-historical events, but they do not reveal any secret doctrines; "the 'what' of the gospel will remain absolutely the same."

- What does it mean that Mark goes "beyond the simple immediate truth"? How do Mark's small details help fill in the larger message of his gospel?

  Going beyond the simple and immediate truth does not mean compromising on the truth; rather, it means that the factual and physical events of the gospel point to big-picture spiritual realities that accompany or are fulfilled in Jesus' miracles and earthly ministry. An example is Jesus' healing Peter's mother-in-law, which points to the larger theme of resurrection and helps us to place our faith in Christ and the reality of the resurrection.

- Why is the gospel not one of the "stories that trap us"? What does it do instead?

  The gospel is not a story that traps us because it saves God's people. Dr. Godfrey recounted a story about a woman who said, "There are stories that save us and stories that trap us." The gospel, the historical record of the life of Jesus Christ, is the type of story that liberates us from the stories that we have told ourselves or have been told by others that tend to trap us. The gospel liberates us from falsehood and also sad truths about our lives, setting us free in truth and faith in Christ.

REVIEW QUIZ

1. **B.**
   Mark frequently uses the word "immediately" to transition from one event to another. As Dr. Godfrey noted in the lecture, this is meant to establish an idea of "rapid movement" throughout the entirety of his gospel.

2. **A.**
   While Mark does use Isaiah to imply the fact that Jesus is God and the Lord of the Old Testament, he does so with the help of a quotation from Malachi to explain the relationship between John the Baptist and Jesus.

3. **B.**
   Dr. Godfrey divides Mark into nine sections, following his chiastic method. The first four sections parallel the last four sections, with both centering on a single point. This is completely distinct from our modern sixteen-chapter division.

4. **C.**
   Mark adds the detail of wild animals' being with Jesus in the wilderness to describe how the place where He was tempted was truly a wilderness. The other examples are not found in Mark's gospel.

5. **B.**
   While modern chapter and verse divisions can be helpful, they are a later addition to the Bible to simplify citation. Therefore, neither of these tools was inspired, as the original manuscripts were.

6. **D.**
   Mark is ultimately looking for people to have faith and to be strengthened in their faith in God. Although this is not in opposition to hope, courage, and love, it is more prominently the main goal of his gospel.

2

Gospel Foundations

INTRODUCTION

What does Mark mean by speaking of "the beginning of the gospel" (Mark 1:1)? And how does the start of his gospel affect the way that we should see the rest of this book? In this lesson, Dr. Godfrey lays a strong foundation for the life and ministry of Jesus as found in the gospel of Mark by showing the depth of Mark's structure and his piercing analysis of spiritual truths.

LEARNING GOALS

When you have finished this lesson, you should be able to:

- Understand why the opening section of Mark is a fitting "beginning"
- Explain the concepts of repentance, the gospel, and the kingdom of God

KEY IDEAS

- The gospel is the fulfillment of many long-standing prophecies.
- John's baptism parallels Jesus' message of repentance and faith.
- Jesus' baptism is the central part of the first section of Mark.

REFLECTION & DISCUSSION QUESTIONS

Before the Video

What Do You Think?

Take a moment to answer the following questions. They will prepare you for the lecture.

- What comes to mind when you hear the word *gospel*?
- What significance does Jesus' baptism have? Why do you think Mark places this event at the beginning of his gospel?

Scripture Reading

In those days Jesus came from Nazareth of Galilee and was baptized by John in the Jordan. And when he came up out of the water, immediately he saw the heavens being torn open and the Spirit descending on him like a dove. And a voice came from heaven, "You are my beloved Son; with you I am well pleased."

—Mark 1:9–11

- How does the baptism of Jesus confirm His role as the Messiah?

During the Video

Answer the following questions while you watch the video. They will guide you through the lecture.

God's Kingdom and Gospel *0:00–16:51*

- What does the word *gospel* mean? How does this tie into Mark's theme?
- What does Jesus mean by "the kingdom of God is at hand" (Mark 1:15)?

Baptism and Repentance *16:51–24:32*

- What is repentance?

- Why is baptism applied to a person by someone else? What does this show about forgiveness?

- What is the significance of Mark's using the phrase "torn open" in his account of Jesus' baptism? What does this phrase allude to?

After the Video

Answer the following questions after you have finished the lecture. They will help you identify and summarize the major points.

- What two titles does Mark attribute to Jesus? Which title is the first half of his gospel about? Which title is the second about? Why is this important?

  If you are in a group, have the members discuss which of the names of God that they have encountered in the Bible are comforting to them and why.

- How is repentance "essential in the Christian life"? Is it part of the gospel? Why or why not?

  If you are in a group, have the members discuss how they can better integrate disciplines of repentance into their relationship with God and how they can practice forgiveness in their relationships with others.

- Why does Mark describe John the Baptist in such vivid detail? How does this allude to the Old Testament? How does it relate to Jesus?

  If you are in a group, have the members discuss why it is important that the New Testament and the Old Testament are connected. Ask: Why didn't God send His Son without prior prophecies?

PRAYER

Commit what you have learned from God's Word in this lesson to prayer.

- Praise God for His infinite wisdom and plan for His people.
- Confess the times that you are reluctant to repent of your sins and turn to Christ.
- Thank God for sending you salvation through Christ and in the Holy Spirit.
- Ask God to help you further know His Son both as Christ and as the Son of God.

REVIEW QUIZ

Use these multiple-choice questions to measure what you learned from this lesson.

1. How long did it take until Isaiah's prophecies were fulfilled by Jesus?
   a. A thousand years
   b. Eight hundred years
   c. Six hundred years
   d. Four hundred and eight hundred years, depending on the prophecy

2. According to Dr. Godfrey, repentance is strictly a part of the gospel.
   a. True
   b. False

3. How did Dr. Godfrey describe the biblical teaching on forgiveness?
   a. As "the first part of the Christian life"
   b. As "the beginning of salvation" and "God's ultimate mercy"
   c. As "a necessary reconciliation from outside us"
   d. As "most necessary" and "absolutely essential"

4. Why did the Pharisees not accept John's baptism?
   a. They thought John was a blasphemer.
   b. They could not find John's baptism in the Torah.
   c. They did not see themselves as sinners.
   d. They had their own form of baptism.

5. Where is the center of Mark's first chiasm?
   a. Mark 1:9–11
   b. Mark 1:4–7
   c. Mark 1:8–11
   d. Mark 1:6–8

6. What location is crucial to both the beginning and end of Mark?
   a. Nazareth
   b. Bethlehem
   c. The Decapolis
   d. Galilee

Answer Key—Gospel Foundations

REFLECTION & DISCUSSION QUESTIONS

Before the Video

What Do You Think?

These are personal questions. The answers should be based on your own knowledge and experience.

Scripture Reading

- How does the baptism of Jesus confirm His role as the Messiah?

  Jesus' baptism confirms the fact that He is the Messiah, since God the Father proclaimed that Jesus is His beloved Son. Not only does this confirm that He is the Son of God and thus God's Anointed, but it also marks the start of His messianic ministry.

During the Video

God's Kingdom and Gospel

- What does the word *gospel* mean? How does this tie into Mark's theme?

  Gospel *literally means "good message." The Greek word is* euangelion*;* eu- *means "good," and* angelion *means "message," "word," or "news." Messengers are a theme in the opening of Mark's gospel, so Dr. Godfrey translates* euangelion *as "good message," which hints at the important messengers who preceded the gospel, such as Isaiah, Malachi, and John the Baptist.*

- What does Jesus mean by "the kingdom of God is at hand" (Mark 1:15)?

  The kingdom of God is essentially the reign of Jesus Christ, who is also its King. The kingdom of God arrives with the coming of Christ and is consummated under Christ. When Jesus says, "The time is fulfilled, and the kingdom of God is at hand," He is announcing His, the King's, arrival.

Baptism and Repentance

- What is repentance?

  Repentance is turning away from sin, which signifies a turning of the mind. In repentance, we have to see ourselves as sinners and turn away from our sin toward Christ.

- Why is baptism applied to a person by someone else? What does this show about forgiveness?

  Baptism is applied by one person to another, according to Jesus' institution of the sacrament (Matt. 28:19), which is why Dr. Godfrey notes that "nobody baptizes themselves in the Bible." This fundamentally shows that baptism represents the forgiveness of sins that is found not in oneself but in another.

- What is the significance of Mark's using the phrase "torn open" in his account of Jesus' baptism? What does this phrase allude to?

  Mark uses the phrase "torn open" to vividly describe the nature of the event at Jesus' baptism, but also to allude to Isaiah's cry, "Oh, that you would rend the heavens and come down" (Isa. 64:1), showing that God has indeed come down and torn open the heavens.

After the Video

- What two titles does Mark attribute to Jesus? Which title is the first half of his gospel about? Which title is the second about? Why is this important?

  Mark speaks of Jesus as both the Christ and the Son of God, with the former being the focus of the first half, showing that Jesus is the Christ, and the latter the focus of the second half, showing that He is the Son of God. This is important because it shows two fundamental emphases of Mark's gospel about Jesus' person and work.

- How is repentance "essential in the Christian life"? Is it part of the gospel? Why or why not?

  Repentance is an essential aspect of the Christian life; someone must turn from his sins to God, not only in his conversion but also as a constant practice day in and day out. While repentance is necessary, it is important to distinguish it from the gospel, so that we do not fall into the belief that we contribute to our salvation through our repentance. We repent from our sin, but we turn in faith to the gospel; it is one thing to repent but another thing to believe.

- Why does Mark describe John the Baptist in such vivid detail? How does this allude to the Old Testament? How does it relate to Jesus?

  Mark describes John the Baptist in such a vivid way to position him as a figurative second Elijah. John stands as the messianic herald and the last step before the Christ's coming as prophesied in Malachi 3–4. This further validates Mark's use of Malachi in Mark 1:3 and stands as a bold claim about the nature of Jesus and His ministry—namely, that He is the true Messiah.

REVIEW QUIZ

1. **B.**
   As Dr. Godfrey noted, Isaiah's many prophecies about Christ were not fulfilled until about eight hundred years after his life, based on the classical and historical Christian date of Isaiah's prophecies.

2. **B.**
   "Repentance is not strictly part of the gospel," as Dr. Godfrey stated, distinguishing

between repenting of sins and believing in the gospel as two different acts, but not to downplay the importance of repentance for the Christian.

3. **D.**
   Dr. Godfrey described the biblical teaching on forgiveness in a few ways, with the standout examples being "most necessary" and "absolutely essential." This is in line with the core message of the gospel and the forgiveness found in Christ.

4. **C.**
   The Pharisees did not see themselves as sinners and thus saw no need for John's baptism of repentance for the remission of sins. They believed in their ability to keep the law, when in reality only Jesus was able to keep the law perfectly.

5. **A.**
   The baptism of Jesus in Mark 1:9–11 is the center of Mark's first chiasm and the focal point of the whole section. This is largely because Jesus' ministry begins with His baptism in all four Gospels and because this baptism is the setting for the first divine declaration that Jesus is the Son of God.

6. **D.**
   Galilee is a crucial location to the gospel of Mark. As Dr. Godfrey noted, the first half of this gospel deals with Jesus' ministry in Galilee, which establishes His role as the Christ. This is further supported by the end of the gospel, where Jesus meets His followers in Galilee, showing that the disciples need a repeated lesson about His person and work.

3

The Faithful Preacher

INTRODUCTION

As Jesus began His ministry in Judea, it became clear to many that He was not just an ordinary teacher, but One who spoke with both authority and power. In this lesson, Dr. Godfrey explains that while Christ's ministry attracted much attention, His work was much deeper and far richer than His miracles alone, and they pointed to the reality that He was *the* Messenger with *the* message.

LEARNING GOALS

When you have finished this lesson, you should be able to:

- Understand how Mark presents Jesus' temptation in the wilderness
- Explain how Jesus' miracles and teaching relate to one another
- Identify and analyze more of the subtle themes in Mark's gospel

KEY IDEAS

- The temptation of Christ in Mark's gospel is interwoven with themes from Psalm 91.
- Mark conceives of Jesus' disciples in a very distinct way compared to others who surrounded Jesus during His ministry.
- Jesus' ministry is characterized by a care for others, even and especially on the Sabbath.

REFLECTION & DISCUSSION QUESTIONS

Before the Video

What Do You Think?

Take a moment to answer the following questions. They will prepare you for the lecture.

- What is the significance of Jesus' temptation in the wilderness, and how does it foreshadow His ministry?
- How do you know that Jesus has authority? How should His authority affect your life?

Scripture Reading

And they were all amazed, so that they questioned among themselves, saying, "What is this? A new teaching with authority! He commands even the unclean spirits, and they obey him."

—Mark 1:27

- What is unique about Jesus' ministry? How does His teaching relate to His power over demons?

During the Video

Answer the following questions while you watch the video. They will guide you through the lecture.

The Temptation *0:00–12:29*

- What is another way to translate the phrase "deliver us from evil" in the Lord's Prayer (Matt. 6:13)? How does this connect to Jesus' experience in the wilderness?
- What is the significance of Psalm 91 in relation to Jesus' temptation and the mention of wild animals?

Authority and Teaching *12:29–24:24*

- Where does Jesus begin His ministry and ultimately return? What is that place like?

- How does Jesus prove that He speaks with authority? How does this affect His popularity?

After the Video

Answer the following questions after you have finished the lecture. They will help you identify and summarize the major points.

- Why does Jesus call the disciples "fishers of men" (Mark 1:17)? What does this indicate about their mission and calling?

  If you are in a group, have the members explain how God has called them to humility in different areas of their lives.

- How do the scribes and Pharisees differ from Jesus in terms of teaching authority? Discuss how Dr. Godfrey contrasted their approach with Jesus' method.

  If you are in a group, ask the members why we should be careful to rely on Christ's authority and God's Word and not elevate the role of men's teaching.

- How are Jesus' healings important to His budding ministry?

  If you are in a group, have the members discuss the importance of Jesus' miracles. Ask: What do Jesus' signs reveal to us about His person?

PRAYER

Commit what you have learned from God's Word in this lesson to prayer.

- Praise God for His sovereign authority over all creation.
- Confess the areas in which you have struggled to submit to your calling as a disciple.
- Thank God for the ways that He has renewed you through the Holy Spirit.
- Ask God to keep you from evil and guide you out of temptation.

REVIEW QUIZ

Use these multiple-choice questions to measure what you learned from this lesson.

1. How does Mark vividly describe the transition from Jesus' baptism to the wilderness?
   a. "Immediately, he went out to the wilderness"
   b. "And Jesus departed to the wilderness, with the wild animals"
   c. "The Spirit immediately drove him out into the wilderness"
   d. "And the Spirit sent him into the wilderness"
2. What two groups does Mark divide Jesus' followers into?
   a. Apostles and followers
   b. Disciples and followers
   c. Apostles and disciples
   d. Followers and believers
3. The synagogue at which Jesus preached in Capernaum is *not* still standing.
   a. True
   b. False
4. What type of event did Dr. Godfrey mention that has a chiastic structure in this section of Mark?
   a. Healing on the Sabbath
   b. Baptism for the remission of sins
   c. Preaching in the synagogue
   d. Going out to a deserted place
5. What are two subtle themes in Mark that Dr. Godfrey said occur "again and again"?
   a. Eating and drinking
   b. Women in Jesus' ministry and becoming fishers of men
   c. Eating and women in Jesus' ministry
   d. Eating and becoming fishers of men
6. Why did people flock to Jesus during His earthly ministry?
   a. People were seeking salvation from their sin and misery.
   b. People were enthralled by His teaching and preaching.
   c. People were interested in the message to which His miraculous power pointed.
   d. People were solely interested in His miraculous power.

Answer Key—The Faithful Preacher

REFLECTION & DISCUSSION QUESTIONS

Before the Video

What Do You Think?

These are personal questions. The answers should be based on your own knowledge and experience.

Scripture Reading

- What is unique about Jesus' ministry? How does His teaching relate to His power over demons?

  Jesus' ministry has an inherent authority that the Jewish people immediately recognize. His teaching and its authority are confirmed by the signs that He works in the synagogue. His casting out demons is a clear sign that His teaching is fully authoritative.

During the Video

The Temptation

- What is another way to translate the phrase "deliver us from evil" in the Lord's Prayer (Matt. 6:15)? How does this connect to Jesus' experience in the wilderness?

  The phrase "deliver us from evil" could be translated "deliver us from the evil one," which, as Dr. Godfrey mentions, links back to Christ's temptation in the wilderness. This translation emphasizes that Jesus, who faced the evil one directly, teaches His followers to pray for protection from such trials. It is as if Jesus is helping us avoid the temptation that He had to suffer.

- What is the significance of Psalm 91 in relation to Jesus' temptation and the mention of wild animals?

  Psalm 91 is one of the passages that Satan used against Jesus in the temptation. This psalm, which speaks of the angels' protecting the faithful, implies that the angels protected Jesus from the wild animals and other natural dangers that were present.

Authority and Teaching

- Where does Jesus begin His ministry and ultimately return? What is that place like?

  Jesus begins His ministry in Capernaum and eventually returns there. Capernaum is a small city near the Sea of Galilee, about twenty-five miles from Nazareth, and is overall not notable because of its size.

- How does Jesus prove that He speaks with authority? How does this affect His popularity?

  Jesus proves that He speaks with authority by casting out a demon, which is an extraordinary miracle. This miracle, meant to testify to His teaching, causes many to seek Jesus as a healer alone.

After the Video

- Why does Jesus call the disciples "fishers of men" (Mark 1:17)? What does this indicate about their mission and calling?

  Jesus calls the disciples "fishers of men" because, though they are given a calling by Jesus, it is not an inherently glorious one. Their title indicates that their mission is not to seek personal glory or wealth but to spread the gospel and draw people to God. They are called to a life of lowliness and suffering for the sake of Christ.

- How do the scribes and Pharisees differ from Jesus in terms of teaching authority? Discuss how Dr. Godfrey contrasted their approach with Jesus' method.

  The scribes and Pharisees would often teach by citing various rabbis. They were invoking not their own authority or the authority of God's Word, but rather the authority of other men. This is distinct from Jesus' authority, which is itself divine and testifies to itself. Jesus did not appeal to the teaching of fallible men but was Himself the infallible Word.

- How are Jesus' healings important to His budding ministry?

  Jesus' healings are important aspects of His ministry as a witness to His very nature. Both men and spirits recognize who He is; it provokes some to see the greater truth that Christ preaches but others to see Jesus as a mere showman. Ultimately, these healings, described by Dr. Godfrey as "mini-resurrections," point to the major theme of the full resurrection that is to come, a complete renewal of both body and soul.

REVIEW QUIZ

1. **C.**
   In Mark 1:12, the Scripture describes this transition as both dramatic, in that Jesus is thrust out, and immediate, to build onto the rapid pace of this gospel. This illustrates what Dr. Godfrey called the "cost of the fulfillment" that must take place in Jesus' life.

2. **B.**
   Mark uses the words "disciples" and "followers" to distinguish between two groups of people that accompanied Jesus. The twelve "disciples" follow Jesus in faith, and

this term can be understood as synonymous with "Apostles." "Followers," for Mark, refers to anyone else who followed Jesus, whether in faith or not.

3. **A.**
   The original synagogue in Capernaum where Jesus preached is no longer standing, but instead it lies under ruins amassed over the centuries.

4. **A.**
   Dr. Godfrey noted that the casting out of the unclean spirit, a healing event, is mirrored later by another healing, both of which take place on the Sabbath day. These events are the second and penultimate features of the chiasm.

5. **C.**
   The themes of eating and women in Jesus' ministry are two examples of repetitive themes in Mark's gospel. These serve to show both the scope and the nature of Jesus' communion with others in His ministry. In many ways, His ministry dealt with the ordinary affairs of everyday people, and He showed a deep care for them in a variety of ways.

6. **D.**
   The main reason why people flocked to Jesus was so that He could heal them or their companions. While some certainly appreciated His preaching, that was not the concern of most, to the point that the crowds diminished when the miracles did.

4

Your Sins Are Forgiven

INTRODUCTION

As Jesus encounters many different types of people in Galilee, He preaches with profound wisdom and performs new miracles. But what characterizes the heart of Jesus' interaction with His followers? In this lesson, Dr. Godfrey expands on the character of Jesus in His encounters with others, emphasizing the centrality of forgiveness and the depth of Christ's compassion.

LEARNING GOALS

When you have finished this lesson, you should be able to:

- Understand how Jesus' healings are not only physically transformative but also socially extraordinary
- Explain how Jesus' interactions with sinners and outcasts reveal the heart of the gospel
- Recognize how Jesus' ministry is marked by compassion and obedience

KEY IDEAS

- The most important healing that Jesus gives is the forgiveness of sins.
- Jesus displays "mini-resurrections" in both His physical healings and His spiritual callings.
- The tensions over fasting and feasting reflect the newness of Jesus' ministry in ushering in the kingdom of God.

REFLECTION & DISCUSSION QUESTIONS

Before the Video

What Do You Think?

Take a moment to answer the following questions. They will prepare you for the lecture.

- Why is it crucial to acknowledge our sin before God? How does repentance relate to forgiveness?

- How should Christians balance fasting and feasting? How can we pursue righteousness without falling into legalism?

Scripture Reading

"Which is easier, to say to the paralytic, 'Your sins are forgiven,' or to say, 'Rise, take up your bed and walk'? But that you may know that the Son of Man has authority on earth to forgive sins"—he said to the paralytic—"I say to you, rise, pick up your bed, and go home."

—Mark 2:9–11

- What does this event reveal about Jesus' authority over both body and soul?

During the Video

Answer the following questions while you watch the video. They will guide you through the lecture.

Healing and Forgiveness *0:00–15:27*

- How does the leper give Jesus both a physical and a social challenge?

- What is the ultimate sickness that Jesus seeks to heal?

- How does Mark show that Jesus is divine in His interaction with the paralytic? Why doesn't he explicitly say so?

Food and Fasting *15:27–24:07*

- What did Jesus do with the tax collectors and sinners that was considered unclean? Why was it supposedly unclean?

- What is the message of the parable of the wineskins?

After the Video

Answer the following questions after you have finished the lecture. They will help you identify and summarize the major points.

- How does the cleansing of the leper show conformity to the law of Moses? How does it also show the compassion of Christ?

  If you are in a group, ask the members how they can abide by the law of God while also showing compassion to others.

- How do the healing and forgiveness of the paralytic parallel Jesus' death and resurrection?

  If you are in a group, have several of the members give an example of how they have been sanctified by Jesus' work in their lives.

- Why is it important to recognize that we are sinners? What should we do after we recognize this?

  If you are in a group, ask the members what attitude they should have in repentance and what attitude they should have in response to forgiveness.

PRAYER

Commit what you have learned from God's Word in this lesson to prayer.

- Praise God for His mighty power to heal us both physically and spiritually.
- Confess any ways that you have neglected to see your need for forgiveness.
- Thank God for sending His Son and Spirit to heal you from the wounds of sin.
- Ask God for the strength to fast from worldly desires and to seek the things that are above.

REVIEW QUIZ

Use these multiple-choice questions to measure what you learned from this lesson.

1. What event is the center of this lesson's chiasm?
   a. The healing of the leper
   b. The feast with the tax collectors
   c. The calling of Levi
   d. The healing of the paralytic

2. From whom does the first human opposition to Jesus' ministry come?
   a. The scribes
   b. The Pharisees
   c. The Sadducees
   d. The Roman soldiers

3. Jesus heard His enemies whisper that He was a blasphemer.
   a. True
   b. False

4. What expression did Mark use to show a mini-resurrection in the calling of Levi?
   a. "He took up his mat and went home."
   b. "He rose and followed."
   c. "He went up to Jesus and followed him."
   d. "He packed up and followed."

5. The only mandated fast in the Old Testament law is for what occasion?
   a. The Feast of Booths
   b. The Passover
   c. The Feast of Purim
   d. The Day of Atonement

6. Why do Jesus and His disciples not fast?
   a. Because Jesus' ministry was opposite of the Pharisees'
   b. Because fasting was for the Old Testament
   c. Because Jesus the King was present with them
   d. Because the disciples required sustenance

Answer Key—Your Sins Are Forgiven

REFLECTION & DISCUSSION QUESTIONS

Before the Video

What Do You Think?

These are personal questions. The answers should be based on your own knowledge and experience.

Scripture Reading

- What does this event reveal about Jesus' authority over both body and soul?

  Jesus has divine authority over both body and soul. By healing the paralytic, He demonstrates His power over the physical. But more significantly, Jesus' authority to forgive sins shows that He has the ultimate power over the soul. By asking which is easier—healing or forgiving—Jesus reveals that while physical healing is miraculous, forgiveness is the far greater and more profound act.

During the Video

Healing and Forgiveness

- How does the leper give Jesus both a physical and a social challenge?

  The leper presents a dual challenge to Jesus: physically, because leprosy was an incurable and highly feared disease; and socially, because lepers were ritually unclean and ostracized from society.

- What is the ultimate sickness that Jesus seeks to heal?

  The ultimate sickness that Jesus seeks to heal is sin. Jesus' greatest gift is forgiveness. While physical illnesses affect the body, sin affects the soul, leading to eternal condemnation. Jesus' primary mission is to save people from sin, which is why He forgives the paralytic before healing him physically.

- How does Mark show that Jesus is divine in His interaction with the paralytic? Why doesn't he explicitly say so?

  Mark indicates that Jesus is divine because He does the very thing that the scribes say that only God can do: forgive sins. As Dr. Godfrey suggests, Mark does not explicitly say that Jesus is God for the same reason that he does not explain his theologically rich prologue: he wants the reader to make the necessary connections.

Food and Fasting

- What did Jesus do with the tax collectors and sinners that was considered unclean? Why was it supposedly unclean?

  Jesus sat at table and feasted with the tax collectors and sinners, which was considered culturally unclean. This was culturally taboo because the Jewish teaching at that time prohibited communion with gentiles and was seen as a defilement of one's own purity.

- What is the message of the parable of the wineskins?

  The newness of Jesus' ministry can be understood in light of the coming of God's kingdom. The parable of the wineskins teaches that the old must not be confused with the new, for the old was passing away, Jesus being its fulfillment.

After the Video

- How does the cleansing of the leper show conformity to the law of Moses? How does it also show the compassion of Christ?

  The cleansing of the leper shows Jesus' conformity to the law of Moses because He instructs the healed leper to go to the priest and offer the sacrifices required for cleansing (Lev. 13:6). Jesus also shows compassion on the leper by touching him to heal him. Touching would ordinarily cause uncleanness or infection, but Jesus does it out of pity for the man and as a demonstration of His power.

- How do the healing and forgiveness of the paralytic parallel Jesus' death and resurrection?

  The paralytic's forgiveness and healing parallel Jesus' death and resurrection in two ways. First, the forgiveness of the paralytic's sins corresponds to Jesus' work on the cross, where He accomplished the paralytic's internal justification. Second, the paralytic's outward healing parallels the external vindication of Christ in His resurrection. The healing shows the inward reality present within the paralytic.

- Why is it important to recognize that we are sinners? What should we do after we recognize this?

  It is vital to recognize that we are sinners because Christ came to save sinners, not the righteous. After becoming conscious of our sins, we ought to accept the great gift of forgiveness through repentance and faith in Christ, just as the paralytic did. Only in humility and lament over our sins can we truly repent of them and cast them on Christ.

REVIEW QUIZ

1. **D.**
   The healing of the paralytic is the center of this lesson's chiasm, which puts a par-

ticular emphasis on this scene as the focus of the surrounding events, highlighting Jesus' authority to forgive sins.

2. **A.**
   The scribes are the first group to oppose Jesus and His ministry. This is not purely external but comes from the internal hostility of their hearts toward Him.

3. **B.**
   Jesus did not hear the scribes speak out against Him, but instead He perceived that they "thus questioned within themselves" (Mark 2:8). This was not an expressed outward doubt but an inward one.

4. **B.**
   After Jesus called Levi, "he rose and followed" (Mark 2:14), which is seemingly insignificant but really shows another instance of Mark's mini-resurrection motif, which is scattered throughout his gospel.

5. **D.**
   The only mandated fast in the Old Testament is on the Day of Atonement (Lev. 23:27–28). This is because the Day of Atonement occupied a central role in Levitical law, which is manifest in the fact that it is the center of a chiasm spanning the whole Pentateuch.

6. **C.**
   Jesus' disciples do not fast because they are with the Bridegroom, Jesus the King. Because the Messiah has come, they are not to fast but rather to celebrate. This does not do away with the validity of fasting; then, it was not fasting time but feasting time.

5

The Care of the Lord of the Sabbath

INTRODUCTION

The fourth commandment was fundamental to the lives of the Israelites, but how are Christians meant to view the Sabbath today? And how did Jesus understand the Sabbath? In this lesson, Dr. Godfrey explains Jesus' view of the Sabbath and His opposition to the legalistic tradition of the Pharisees, ultimately showing how Christians are to perceive the fourth commandment today.

LEARNING GOALS

When you have finished this lesson, you should be able to:

- Understand the biblical view of the Sabbath and its purpose for us
- Explain how the Pharisees misused tradition and misunderstood the law
- Identify the different groups that followed Jesus and their motives

KEY IDEAS

- The Sabbath is made for man to rest in God and enjoy His gifts.
- The ceremonial law could be broken out of necessity; it was never intended to be a rigid, lifeless system that burdened people.
- Jesus, as God, is Lord of the Sabbath, with authority to interpret and fulfill it.

REFLECTION & DISCUSSION QUESTIONS

Before the Video

What Do You Think?

Take a moment to answer the following questions. They will prepare you for the lecture.

- Should Christians still observe the Sabbath today? Why or why not?

- When does tradition go too far in distorting the law? How should Christians view tradition?

Scripture Reading

And he said to them, "The Sabbath was made for man, not man for the Sabbath. So the Son of Man is lord even of the Sabbath."

—Mark 2:27–28

- What does it mean that the Sabbath was made for man and not man for the Sabbath?

During the Video

Answer the following questions while you watch the video. They will guide you through the lecture.

The Sabbath and Necessity *0:00–15:44*

- To what degree did the Pharisees believe that Jesus had broken the law?

- What is the ultimate purpose of the Sabbath? What does Isaiah say is the proper attitude toward the Sabbath?

- What does Jesus' divinity have to do with His authority over the Sabbath?

The Sabbath and Mercy *15:44–23:52*

- Do the Pharisees know that it is lawful to save life on the Sabbath? Why or why not?

- How do the Pharisees react to Jesus' performing acts of mercy on the Sabbath?

After the Video

Answer the following questions after you have finished the lecture. They will help you identify and summarize the major points.

- What is an *a fortiori* argument? How does Jesus use this type of argument to challenge the Pharisees' understanding of the law?

  If you are in a group, ask the members discuss what is the problem with the Pharisees' understanding of the law and provide examples from their knowledge of the Gospels.

- What is the right understanding of the Sabbath? Should Christians abolish or continue to observe the Sabbath? Why?

  If you are in a group, ask the members whether they observe the Sabbath and, if so, how. Ask: How are Christians supposed to rest in God?

- For whose sake should we follow Jesus and observe the Sabbath?

  If you are in a group, have the members explain how they started following Jesus and for what reason. Ask: Why do you follow Him now?

PRAYER

Commit what you have learned from God's Word in this lesson to prayer.

- Praise God for His mercy and steadfast care for His covenant people.
- Confess the areas in your life where you rest in worldly things instead of in Christ.
- Thank God for providing a Sabbath rest in Christ both now and in the age to come.
- Ask God to empower you by His Spirit to rest more deeply in Him and to trust Him for all things.

REVIEW QUIZ

Use these multiple-choice questions to measure what you learned from this lesson.

1. The Mosaic law allowed people to glean wheat on the Sabbath.
   a. True
   b. False
2. What literary device is Jesus using when He says, "Have you never read what David did?" (Mark 2:25)?
   a. Synecdoche
   b. Comedy
   c. Irony
   d. Hyperbole
3. When was the Sabbath instituted?
   a. Immediately after the fall
   b. With the Mosaic law
   c. With the Abrahamic covenant
   d. During creation
4. After refuting the Pharisees, how did Jesus look at the Pharisees?
   a. With anger
   b. With pity
   c. With disappointment
   d. With love
5. What psalm does Mark allude to in the withered-hand narrative?
   a. Psalm 1
   b. Psalm 2
   c. Psalm 22
   d. Psalm 23
6. What kind of people started following Jesus around at this point in His ministry?
   a. Roman soldiers
   b. Pharisees and demons
   c. Herodians
   d. Pharisees and Sadducees

Answer Key—The Care of the Lord of the Sabbath

REFLECTION & DISCUSSION QUESTIONS

Before the Video

What Do You Think?

These are personal questions. The answers should be based on your own knowledge and experience.

Scripture Reading

- What does it mean that the Sabbath was made for man and not man for the Sabbath?

  The Sabbath's being made for man implies that it serves us because we were not created for the Sabbath; rather, it is the other way around: the Sabbath was created for us. It is to serve a spiritual and physical benefit to us. In contrast, if we understand man to have been made for the Sabbath, we run the risk of turning its observance into a burden.

During the Video

The Sabbath and Necessity

- To what degree did the Pharisees believe that Jesus had broken the law?

  The Pharisees thought that Jesus had broken not only the customary law that their tradition upheld but also the full commandment of the Mosaic law itself. This means that they perceived Him as being a lawbreaker to the highest degree, despite violating only their tradition.

- What is the ultimate purpose of the Sabbath? What does Isaiah say is the proper attitude toward the Sabbath?

  The ultimate purpose of the Sabbath is to be an encouragement, blessing, and rest to the people of God. Because this is such a significant gift to mankind, Isaiah says that the proper attitude is to "call the Sabbath a delight" (Isa. 58:13).

- What does Jesus' divinity have to do with His authority over the Sabbath?

  Jesus' divinity is central because, as the Son of God, He created the Sabbath, and as its Creator, He knows exactly what it entails. This is the striking claim that He is making when He says, "The Son of Man is lord even of the Sabbath" (Mark 2:28).

The Sabbath and Mercy

- Do the Pharisees know that it is lawful to save life on the Sabbath? Why or why not?

  The Pharisees know that it is lawful to save life on the Sabbath because Moses said this much (see Deut. 22:4). The Mosaic law allows for this as an exception out of mercy, and since the Pharisees knew these principles thoroughly, they were completely aware that healing and helping is not only lawful, but also obligatory.

- How do the Pharisees react to Jesus' performing acts of mercy on the Sabbath?

  Contrary to the Mosaic law's intent, the Pharisees desire to condemn Jesus for His act of mercy toward the man with the withered hand. They want not only to prosecute Him but also to sentence Him to death, which is why Mark records that they seek "how to destroy him" (3:6).

After the Video

- What is an *a fortiori* argument? How does Jesus use this type of argument to challenge the Pharisees' understanding of the law?

  An a fortiori *argument is a form of logical argumentation in which a lesser term is proved true by a greater term or principle. Jesus uses this type of argument when He appeals to David's eating the bread of the Presence in 1 Samuel 21 as an act of necessity. This validates the lesser example of His disciples' picking grain out of a similar need for food.*

- What is the right understanding of the Sabbath? Should Christians abolish or continue to observe the Sabbath? Why?

  The right understanding of the Sabbath is the consecration of one day out of seven fully to God. For the Israelites, this meant the last day of the week (Ex. 20:8–11), but for Christians, this corresponds to the first day of the week because of Christ's resurrection (Acts 20:7; Rev. 1:10). The Sabbath is not to be abolished but is to be celebrated anew in Christ because He is our true Sabbath rest.

- For whose sake should we follow Jesus and observe the Sabbath?

  We should observe the Sabbath and follow Jesus for His sake. The motive behind both these actions should be guided not by selfish ambition but by the love of God, which is both to believe in Christ (John 6:29) and to keep His commandments (14:15).

REVIEW QUIZ

1. **A.**
   The Mosaic law did permit gleaning on the edge of a field, which is why Ruth did so at Boaz's field to help provide for both her and Naomi. The Mosaic law had measures to provide for those in need of food or who were just hungry (Deut. 23:25;

24:19–22). The Pharisees had expanded the Sabbath prohibition against work to the degree that it effectively canceled out these measures.

2. **C.**
   Here, Jesus is using irony to show the absurdity of the Pharisees' position on the Sabbath. Irony deals with the difference between appearance and reality. Jesus asks a question that seems genuine, but really serves to show how the Pharisees, who are familiar with the Old Testament, are acting as though they have never read it.

3. **D.**
   The Sabbath was given at creation, as seen in the beginning of Genesis 2 on the seventh day. This is why the Sabbath is not grounded on an act of God in the Mosaic covenant but rather is based on the created order of the world (Ex. 20:11).

4. **A.**
   Jesus looked at the Pharisees with anger because He knew their true intentions and heart. They claimed to be experts in the law, but as Dr. Godfrey stated, they were "so hardened" that they could not understand it. While Jesus was also grieved at the situation (Mark 3:5), the text does not say that He looked at them with pity.

5. **B.**
   The withered-hand narrative points to Psalm 2, for the Pharisees plot in vain against the Lord's Anointed. Just as the nations take counsel against the Christ in Psalm 2, so too do the Pharisees and Herodians formulate a plot against Jesus.

6. **B.**
   At this point in Jesus' ministry, not only do His friends follow Him around, but also His enemies. As Dr. Godfrey mentioned, now the Pharisees and demons began following Jesus to work against Him and His ministry.

6

The Apostles and Lessons on Rejection

INTRODUCTION

Throughout Jesus' ministry, He encountered significant opposition and rejection. How did He respond to these challenges, and who are truly considered His followers? In this lesson, Dr. Godfrey explores the foundational role of the Apostles in the Christian church and explains what it means to truly be a part of Christ's spiritual family.

LEARNING GOALS

When you have finished this lesson, you should be able to:

- Identify the unique role of the Apostles
- Describe Jesus' response to His opposition and rejection
- Understand the purpose and function of parables in Jesus' ministry

KEY IDEAS

- The Apostles were called not because of anything special in them, but because they were specially entrusted with carrying on the work of building Christ's church after He was gone.
- Jesus did not seek earthly power or success; instead, His ministry was characterized by suffering for the kingdom of God, as would be the case for His disciples.
- In Mark 3, Jesus faces the rejection of both His family and the renowned scribes of His day.

REFLECTION & DISCUSSION QUESTIONS

Before the Video

What Do You Think?

Take a moment to answer the following questions. They will prepare you for the lecture.

- Why did Jesus call the Apostles? What sets them apart from His other followers?
- What is blasphemy against the Holy Spirit? Can a Christian commit this sin?

Scripture Reading

"If Satan has risen up against himself and is divided, he cannot stand, but is coming to an end. But no one can enter a strong man's house and plunder his goods, unless he first binds the strong man. Then indeed he may plunder his house."

—Mark 3:28

- Who is the strong man? Why is it important for Jesus to bind him?

During the Video

Answer the following questions while you watch the video. They will guide you through the lecture.

Calling of the Apostles *0:00–9:05*

- What does the phrase "one holy catholic and Apostolic church" mean?
- What kind of authority did Jesus give to the Apostles?

Power and Parables *9:05–24:35*

- Why did Jesus' family reject Him initially? Did they later change their attitude?
- What is the relation of Jesus' ministry to earthly success?

After the Video

Answer the following questions after you have finished the lecture. They will help you identify and summarize the major points.

- How did the early Protestants lay claim to Apostolic authority? How is this different from the Roman Catholic view of Apostolic succession?

  If you are in a group, have the members discuss whether they consider the Apostolic office as an enduring office. Ask: What is the importance of the Apostles to Christian theology?

- How does Jesus speak of His family? What does He imply is more important than a biological relationship to Him?

  If you are in a group, have the members explain how they know that they are in a relationship with Jesus.

- What is blasphemy against the Holy Spirit? Why is it unforgivable?

  If you are in a group, have the members discuss why the Holy Spirit is important to Jesus' life and ministry and in what way the Spirit and Jesus are inseparable, such that speaking against Jesus' works is speaking against the Spirit.

PRAYER

Commit what you have learned from God's Word in this lesson to prayer.

- Praise God for His mighty power in establishing His kingdom.
- Confess the times you have neglected your calling as a disciple.
- Thank God for the gift of the Holy Spirit, who empowers you to live according to God's will.
- Ask God to give you the eyes to see yourself and other Christians as a true spiritual family in Christ.

REVIEW QUIZ

Use these multiple-choice questions to measure what you learned from this lesson.

1. What authority does Peter tell us to follow in 1 Peter?
   a. The Apostolic bishops
   b. The governing authority
   c. The witness of miracles
   d. The Word of God

2. We do not have a lot of information about each Apostle.
   a. True
   b. False

3. How do we know that the scribes in Mark 3 were important figures?
   a. Because they came from Jerusalem
   b. Because Mark explicitly mentions their importance
   c. Because they were faithful expositors of the Scriptures
   d. Both a and b

4. How does Jesus refute the scribes' claim that He had a demon?
   a. He appeals to the Scriptures.
   b. He shows that it is absurd.
   c. He performs a miracle.
   d. He uses a logical syllogism.

5. What is the key question in the issue of blasphemy against the Holy Spirit?
   a. Does the Holy Spirit proceed from Jesus?
   b. Are miracles from the Holy Spirit?
   c. Is the Holy Spirit real?
   d. What Spirit is in Jesus?

6. What is the main reason that Jesus communicated in parables?
   a. Because they were easy to remember
   b. Because they were difficult to remember
   c. So that most people would understand them
   d. So that most people would not understand them

Answer Key—The Apostles and Lessons on Rejection

REFLECTION & DISCUSSION QUESTIONS

Before the Video

What Do You Think?

These are personal questions. The answers should be based on your own knowledge and experience.

Scripture Reading

- Who is the strong man? Why is it important for Jesus to bind him?

  The strong man represents Satan. Jesus must bind him so that He can plunder from Satan his spiritual dominion. The coming of the kingdom of God is marked by the casting out of demons (Luke 11:20), and we will see that the accusation that Jesus is demon-possessed is ridiculous, for then Satan would be against himself through Jesus' ministry of casting out demons.

During the Video

Calling of the Apostles

- What does the phrase "one holy catholic and Apostolic church" mean?

  The phrase "one holy catholic and Apostolic church," from the Nicene Creed, simply means that Christ established a single church, united to Himself as its head (Col. 2:19), who nourishes the whole body. The church is holy and has been sanctified and set apart by God and for God (Eph. 5:26). It was established through the Apostles and is universal, or "catholic," because it is throughout the world.

- What kind of authority did Jesus give to the Apostles?

  Jesus gave the Apostles His own miraculous authority. As those with a direct extension of Christ's own power, they were able to do all the signs that He did—namely, healing and casting out demons to display Christ's authority.

Power and Parables

- Why did Jesus' family reject Him initially? Did they later change their attitude?

  Jesus' family rejected Him because, like the people around them, they could not understand who He truly was. Even though His mother, Mary, knew that Jesus was special, He made claims that startled even her. Despite her initial hesitation, eventually Mary came around to Jesus' teaching, and tradition identifies His brother James as leader of the Jerusalem church and the same man who wrote the epistle of James.

- What is the relation of Jesus' ministry to earthly success?

  One of the major points that Mark notes about Jesus' ministry is that it was not about earthly or worldly success. This is seen first in how he records Christ's calling His disciples to be fishers of men; they were not the elites of society. Jesus' ministry instead echoes the words to them, "Don't expect success now," showing how Jesus' message and work was a gospel of suffering and not a gospel of success.

After the Video

- How did the early Protestants lay claim to Apostolic authority? How is this different from the Roman Catholic view of Apostolic succession?

  The early Protestants and Reformers saw Apostolicity not as a succession of holy orders, but rather as conformity to the purity of the Apostolic doctrine, which is found only in the teaching of Scripture. The Roman Catholic view, on the other hand, emphasized the physical descent of ordination from bishop to bishop.

- How does Jesus speak of His family? What does He imply is more important than a biological relationship to Him?

  Jesus speaks of His family in spiritual terms and not earthly ones, and in a sense does not speak of His physical family as His proper family. Instead, Christ says that His true family are those who do the will of God. By saying this, Jesus implies that doing the will of God is more important than any biological relationship that His mother and brothers have to Him.

- What is blasphemy against the Holy Spirit? Why is it unforgivable?

  Blasphemy against the Holy Spirit is what Dr. Godfrey also called the "eternal sin" because it consists of perpetually denying that Christ has the Spirit of God, instead calling His work the work of the devil. This sin is unforgivable because it is absolutely incompatible with faith in Jesus as the Christ.

REVIEW QUIZ

1. **D.**
   Peter calls his audience to hold fast to the Word of God in the first chapter of his epistle. He describes it as "the living and abiding word of God" (1 Peter 1:23). Moreover, Peter exhorts the elders "as a fellow elder" (5:1), which shows that his emphasis is not on an invested episcopal or Apostolic authority, but rather on the Word of God.

2. **A.**
   While we know much about Peter, John, and other notable Apostles in the New Testament, some (such as Simon the Zealot) are less well documented and no more than a name in the Gospels.

3. **A.**
The scribes were notable figures because they had prominent urban positions and consequently much power over the religious lives of the ordinary Jews. While they would have dealt with the Scriptures on a regular basis, they were unfaithful in interpreting them because they conflated the work of the Christ with the work of Beelzebub.

4. **B.**
Christ refutes the scribes' claim that He was demon-possessed by showing the absurdity of such a position. Since casting out demons weakened Satan's hold on the world, Jesus could not be operating on demonic authority, for then Satan would be establishing his kingdom by simultaneously tearing it down.

5. **D.**
As Dr. Godfrey noted in the lecture, the fundamental question that blasphemy against the Holy Spirit addresses is this: What Spirit is in Jesus? While this does encompass the reality of the Holy Spirit and His miraculous work, those issues are less central to the question of blasphemy.

6. **D.**
Contrary to popular belief, Jesus did not teach in parables so that people could better remember or understand them. Though parables were a helpful and memorable storytelling technique, this was not Christ's main objective in speaking in parables. Rather, it was to see who would seek to know the real meaning behind the parables (see Mark 4:10–12).

7

Lessons about Kingdom Growth

INTRODUCTION

Jesus spoke in many parables, some of which are clearer than others, but why did He speak in this manner, and what do the parables ultimately mean? In this lesson, Dr. Godfrey explores the meaning of some of Jesus' most popular parables, focusing on how they reveal truths about the nature of the kingdom of God and the spiritual condition of those who hear them.

LEARNING GOALS

When you have finished this lesson, you should be able to:

- Identify the meaning of multiple parables from Mark 4
- Understand Jesus' teaching on the character and growth of the kingdom of God
- Explain the relationship of faith and fear as the disciples followed Jesus

KEY IDEAS

- The parables are intentionally cryptic, designed to reveal and conceal, based on the condition of the hearer's heart.
- The kingdom of God grows mysteriously and often, for a time, may go unnoticed.
- Followers of Jesus are called to live by faith, even in the face of fear.

REFLECTION & DISCUSSION QUESTIONS

Before the Video

What Do You Think?

Take a moment to answer the following questions. They will prepare you for the lecture.

- What does the Word of God bring to those who hear it? Why should we continue to share the Word with others even if it is rejected?

- How does the kingdom of God expand? How does it begin?

Scripture Reading

And he awoke and rebuked the wind and said to the sea, "Peace! Be still!" And the wind ceased, and there was a great calm. He said to them, "Why are you so afraid? Have you still no faith?" And they were filled with great fear and said to one another, "Who then is this, that even the wind and the sea obey him?"

—Mark 4:39–41

- What other question like this one have we encountered from the gospel of Mark that is meant to communicate something to us about Jesus' full identity? What does this question communicate about it?

During the Video

Answer the following questions while you watch the video. They will guide you through the lecture.

The Sower *0:00–12:38*

- What theme from the previous lesson does the parable of the sower elaborate on? How so?

- What is a sign that faith has no root and is not genuine?

The Storm *12:38–24:52*

- What is the moral of the parable of the lamp and the basket?

- Why does Jesus use a mustard seed as an analogy of the kingdom of God?

- What is the relationship of faith to fear? Which one best describes the disciples in the storm and why?

After the Video

Answer the following questions after you have finished the lecture. They will help you identify and summarize the major points.

- What response is Jesus trying to elicit through the parables? Why?

  If you are in a group, ask the members what confuses them about Jesus' parables, but also what they enjoy about them. Ask: How should we approach the parables, knowing that the Holy Spirit indwells us?

- What does each soil represent? What does each soil's reaction to the Word represent?

  If you are in a group, have the members describe which soil most resembled their lives before Christ and why. Have them also describe how God changed their hearts or "soil" from poor to rich.

- What does the storm narrative reveal about Jesus? How does it relate to the Old Testament, and why is that connection important?

  If you are in a group, ask the members how Jesus' calming of the storm allows them to rest in Him. Ask: What trials in your life have most served to show you Jesus' omnipotence and glory?

PRAYER

Commit what you have learned from God's Word in this lesson to prayer.

- Praise God for His providence over all creation, commanding every single detail.
- Confess the places in your life where fear prevails over faith.
- Thank God for sending a true Teacher in His Son, so that you might have life abundantly through what He has revealed.
- Ask God for a firm rooting in His Word and Spirit and for the grace to faithfully steward the Word for others.

REVIEW QUIZ

Use these multiple-choice questions to measure what you learned from this lesson.

1. The Word of God goes forth to bring both salvation and what else?
   a. Sin
   b. Prosperity
   c. Peace
   d. Judgment
2. What did Martin Luther advise his wife to do in circumstances of worry?
   a. "Pray, and let God worry."
   b. "Read the Scriptures and pray."
   c. "Pray, and receive the Lord's Supper."
   d. "Remember Christ's sacrifice for you."
3. We must prepare ourselves to receive the Word.
   a. True
   b. False
4. How does Jesus describe the growth of God's kingdom?
   a. As the growth from a boy to a man
   b. As the mustard seed's size
   c. As a lamp moved from a basket to a stand
   d. As the mystery of a seed growing
5. What connection did Dr. Godfrey make between Jesus' teaching on the Word and His sea trip?
   a. The water symbolizes chaos without the Word.
   b. The water symbolizes the vast expanse that the Word is to be spread over.
   c. The sea trip gives the disciples an opportunity to grow the kingdom elsewhere.
   d. The sea trip gives the disciples an opportunity to believe the Word practically.
6. What type of soil do the disciples imitate during the storm at sea?
   a. The thorny soil
   b. The good soil
   c. The soil on the path
   d. The rocky soil

Answer Key—Lessons about Kingdom Growth

REFLECTION & DISCUSSION QUESTIONS

Before the Video

What Do You Think?

These are personal questions. The answers should be based on your own knowledge and experience.

Scripture Reading

- What other question like this one have we encountered from the gospel of Mark that is meant to communicate something to us about Jesus' full identity? What does this question communicate about it?

  While not stated outright by Mark, this question communicates that Christ is omnipotent, for only the Creator is able to control such things as wind and waves. This is like the question asked in Mark 2: "Who can forgive sins but God alone?" (v. 7).

During the Video

The Sower

- What theme from the previous lesson does the parable of the sower elaborate on? How so?

  The parable of the sower further elaborates on the previous theme of rejection. Just as Jesus and His message were rejected at Nazareth and will be shunned elsewhere, so too do most of the soils prove to ultimately reject the Word, which is the preaching of Christ.

- What is a sign that faith has no root and is not genuine?

  Faith is tested by what a person ultimately values most. While all Christians struggle with sin (1 John 1:8), a persistent placement of the things of this world above the truths of the Word of God reveals a faith without root and not a sincere faith, which Paul praises in 2 Timothy 1:5.

The Storm

- What is the moral of the parable of the lamp and the basket?

  The parable of the lamp and the basket communicates what one ought to do with the Word of God. Christians are not supposed to keep their faith totally private;

rather, they are to let it shine forth as an extension of Christ's light in the world. As Dr. Godfrey succinctly puts it, the moral is that we have a responsibility to bear the Word faithfully.

- Why does Jesus use a mustard seed as an analogy of the kingdom of God?

  Jesus uses the example of the mustard seed to explain the humble origins and grand end of God's kingdom because of its small size and great effect. Even though it is among the smallest of seeds, the large tree that springs forth from it has such an encompassing effect that birds can now perch on it.

- What is the relationship of faith to fear? Which one best describes the disciples in the storm and why?

  Faith and fear are opposites in this narrative. Fear arises when there is a lack of trust, while faith is confidence in God's power and care. The disciples, overwhelmed by the storm, demonstrate fear rather than faith. Jesus rebukes them for their fear, saying: "Why are you so afraid? Have you still no faith?" (Mark 4:40).

After the Video

- What response is Jesus trying to elicit through the parables? Why?

  When Jesus teaches in parables, His goal is to have people ask Him what the meanings of the parables are by expressing legitimate interest in their teachings. Yet He does this, knowing that many will remain hardhearted regardless of this invitation to learn from Him. As Dr. Godfrey noted in Christ's quotation of Isaiah 6, the Word can condemn people for unbelief, just as much as it can likewise be used by the Spirit so that they might be justified through belief.

- What does each soil represent? What does each soil's reaction to the Word represent?

  Each soil represents a different type of hearer of God's Word and the person's reaction to hearing it. The soil on the path represents those who immediately dispose of the Word and yield it to Satan. The rocky soil represents those who hear the Word with a shallow acceptance, and thus they fall away when they are tested. The thorny soil represents those who likewise receive the Word positively but are choked out by the cares of the world. Finally, the good soil represents those who accept the Word in true faith and bear fruit in accordance with it.

- What does the storm narrative reveal about Jesus? How does it relate to the Old Testament, and why is that connection important?

  The storm narrative reveals that Jesus has command of the wind and the sea, ultimately testifying to the fact that He is the One who rules the universe. This relates to Psalm 104, which states, "He makes the clouds his chariot; he rides on the wings of the wind" (v. 3). This statement, applied to God, now alludes to Christ, God in the flesh, so this is an important testimony not only of Christ's power, but of His very divinity.

REVIEW QUIZ

1. **D.**
   As Dr. Godfrey noted, Scripture brings not only salvation but also judgment on those who hear it, depending on how it is received. The people who receive the Word with faith and repentance have received God's grace, but those who shun the Word in the hardness of their hearts are likewise shunned by God in judgment.

2. **A.**
   Martin Luther told his wife to "pray, and let God worry," which does not mean that God worries as we do, but rather means that we are called to cast all our anxieties on Him, for He cares for us (1 Peter 5:7). Despite how tempting it might be to yield to the cares of the world, there is true rest only in the God who cares for us.

3. **B.**
   Although it is important to approach the Word of God with reverence, one is converted to faith by God and not by one's own will, since Christians are called "not because of works but because of him who calls" (Rom. 9:11). Because it is God who works in us, we cannot take ultimate credit for faith and our reception of the Word.

4. **D.**
   While Jesus uses a couple of other parables to describe the kingdom of God, the parable of the growing seed shows how the kingdom of God mysteriously expands ultimately by God's own working to expand it.

5. **D.**
   The sea trip is a practical moment that calls the disciples to faith as it tests their confidence in the words that Jesus has just preached. They have received all the doctrine from their Teacher, but now they have to trust Him, even when other things demand their attention.

6. **A.**
   The disciples are like the thorny soil in the storm narrative because earthly cares choke out their faith in Christ. As Dr. Godfrey remarked, "One might almost say they are overwhelmed by the cares of the world," which is exactly how the seed was choked by the thorns.

8

Deliverance to the Gentiles

INTRODUCTION

After teaching the crowds and the disciples in parables, Jesus went on a brief mission trip to minister among the gentiles. This journey highlights Jesus' authority over nature, demons, and death, revealing both His compassion and His power. In this lesson, Dr. Godfrey shows how Jesus' actions reveal His identity and the nature of His mission, teaching His disciples lessons on faith and deliverance that will shape their future ministry.

LEARNING GOALS

When you have finished this lesson, you should be able to:

- Understand why Jesus made a brief trip to the Gerasenes
- Describe the characteristics of demons as presented in Mark's gospel
- Recognize themes of deliverance, faith, and authority in Jesus' miracles and teachings

KEY IDEAS

- Jesus' mission illustrates His deliverance for all people and is a practical extension of His parables about kingdom growth.
- Faith in God brings true peace and healing.
- Jesus' mission reveals Him to be Lord of life; His authority knows no boundaries, and even death has no sway over Him.

REFLECTION & DISCUSSION QUESTIONS

Before the Video

What Do You Think?

Take a moment to answer the following questions. They will prepare you for the lecture.

- What are demons? What are their objectives?
- Does faith always bring healing? Why or why not?

Scripture Reading

"Why are you making a commotion and weeping? The child is not dead but sleeping." And they laughed at him. But he put them all outside and took the child's father and mother and those who were with him and went in where the child was. Taking her by the hand he said to her, "Talitha cumi," which means, "Little girl, I say to you, arise." And immediately the girl got up and began walking.

—Mark 5:39b–42a

- Why does Jesus say that the girl was sleeping and not dead? What does "sleeping" mean in this context?

During the Video

Answer the following questions while you watch the video. They will guide you through the lecture.

Jesus and Legion *0:00–14:48*

- Why are the tombs a significant setting for Jesus' encounter with Legion?
- Why did the demons rush the swine off a cliff?

Two Healings *14:48–24:52*

- Why was it scandalous for the woman to push through the crowd to reach Jesus? What is Mark assuming of his readers here?

- What was Jesus' response to the ruler of the synagogue when he was told not to trouble Jesus on account of his daughter?

After the Video

Answer the following questions after you have finished the lecture. They will help you identify and summarize the major points.

- What does the Greek word for "apostle" mean? Compare and contrast how the demons and disciples are both apostles.

  If you are in a group, have the members explain how all Christians are, in a sense, sent by God. Ask: What does this mean for our everyday lives?

- How does the demoniac man exemplify how Christians are to share their testimony? How might this affect the hearer?

  If you are in a group, ask the members about a time when their testimony or evangelism fell on good soil. Ask: How did this experience encourage your faith?

- Compare and contrast the healing of the unclean woman with the resurrection of Jairus' daughter. What is significant about the years that were mentioned?

  If you are in a group, have the members explain how different miracles reveal different things about Jesus and His earthly ministry.

PRAYER

Commit what you have learned from God's Word in this lesson to prayer.

- Praise God for His expansive mercy and encompassing love.
- Confess the times in your life when you have disregarded what God could do in your life.
- Thank God for the gift of faith in His Son and the peace that comes from it.
- Ask God for the Spirit to move you to share the gospel with others.

REVIEW QUIZ

Use these multiple-choice questions to measure what you learned from this lesson.

1. What does the location of the Gerasenes reveal about this mission trip?
   a. It was to demon-possessed people.
   b. It was for the ruler's daughter in particular.
   c. It was to the gentiles.
   d. It was to Jewish unbelievers.
2. What remark does Legion make that reveals that demons are self-centered?
   a. "My name is Legion."
   b. "What have you to do with me?"
   c. "Do not torment me."
   d. "Send us to the pigs; let us enter them."
3. Why would the people not receive Jesus after He cast out Legion?
   a. They could not understand Jesus' power.
   b. They were demonically influenced.
   c. They were still afraid of Legion.
   d. They were, metaphorically, bad soil.
4. Jesus does not let the man who was possessed by Legion join Him.
   a. True
   b. False
5. How does Mark describe the manner in which the unclean woman approached Jesus?
   a. "With gratitude and joy"
   b. "In fear and trembling"
   c. "In awe and reverence"
   d. "With doubt and hesitation"
6. What common theme in Mark appears immediately after the resurrection of the young girl?
   a. Women
   b. Eating
   c. Urgency
   d. Faith and fear

Answer Key—Deliverance to the Gentiles

REFLECTION & DISCUSSION QUESTIONS

Before the Video

What Do You Think?

These are personal questions. The answers should be based on your own knowledge and experience.

Scripture Reading

- Why does Jesus say that the girl was sleeping and not dead? What does "sleeping" mean in this context?

  Jesus does not say that she died, because she was not dead beyond all hope of life. Just as John 11 shows with Lazarus, Jesus reveals how physical death foreshadows resurrection, but spiritual death is irreversible. Here, "sleeping" reflects the same impermanence of death, foreshadowing Jesus' resurrection of the girl.

During the Video

Jesus and Legion

- Why are the tombs a significant setting for Jesus' encounter with Legion?

  Tombs are a significant setting for the beginning of this mission trip by virtue of how striking and surprising they are. The encounter with Legion is not set in the typical crowds and towns in which Jesus ordinarily cast out demons. Rather, this is in a strange and eerie location that would have stood out to any of the original readers.

- Why did the demons rush the swine off a cliff?

  We do not know why the demons asked to inhabit the herd of pigs, but they rushed them off a cliff to destroy them. Demons inherently desire death and destruction. We especially see this in the torment of the demon-possessed man.

Two Healings

- Why was it scandalous for the woman to push through the crowd to reach Jesus? What is Mark assuming of his readers here?

  It was scandalous for the woman to push through the crowd because she was ceremonially unclean, meaning that she would contaminate the rest of the crowd and make them unclean by contact. Because of this, Mark assumes that the reader is aware of the Mosaic law concerning this condition and understands the implications of her daring act.

- What was Jesus' response to the ruler of the synagogue when he was told not to trouble Jesus on account of his daughter?

  Jairus had faith in Jesus, but the people from his household thought it was useless to trouble Jesus, for Jairus' daughter had died while he was seeking her healing. Jesus reassured Jairus, "Do not fear, only believe" (Mark 5:36). Just as Jesus Christ prompted His disciples from fear to faith during the storm at sea, He moved Jairus from fear to a deep assurance that Christ was able to raise his daughter from the dead.

After the Video

- What does the Greek word for "apostle" mean? Compare and contrast how the demons and disciples are both apostles.

  The Greek word for "apostle" (apostolos) *means "sent one" or "one who is sent." This helps bring a notable comparison between the demons and the disciples—namely, that they are both sent, but by different masters. The demons are sent by Satan, while the disciples are sent by Christ. Demons seek chaos and destruction, but those sent by Christ seek to bring truth and life.*

- How does the demoniac man exemplify how Christians are to share their testimony? How might this affect the hearer?

  The demoniac man gives an example for all Christians to follow, which is to tell others what the Lord has done. Christians are to be joyous and unapologetic in their witness for Christ, sharing with all those nearby, as the same man went and witnessed to the whole Decapolis (which is ten cities). This could affect someone greatly, perhaps prompting the person to ask, "Could Jesus do such a work in my life?"

- Compare and contrast the healing of the unclean woman with the resurrection of Jairus' daughter. What is significant about the years that were mentioned?

  The two healings during this ministry are unique in that they both reveal Jesus' healing in extreme cases, one physical and another ceremonial. While the woman contracted her disease twelve years before her encounter with Jesus, the girl died at twelve years of age. This connection helps us to see that Jesus is the Lord over all life, no matter what the circumstances are. Many possible connections could be made regarding faith, the completeness of the number twelve, and the action of Jesus, but these are the principal points of comparison.

REVIEW QUIZ

1. **C.**
   The Gerasenes are in a significant location because it is a non-Jewish territory and thus marks the first journey to the gentiles in the gospel of Mark. Jesus' main ministry was to the Jewish people, but His saving work is for both gentiles and Jews

alike (see Gal. 3:28; Eph. 2:14), which is why this place shows an important aspect of His ministry.

2. **C.**
   Legion reveals the self-centered ideology of demons, since their goal is to save themselves and live for themselves. Even though Legion is tormenting the man they possess, they have the audacity to request not to be tormented.

3. **D.**
   Dr. Godfrey explained that the townspeople, though witnessing the miraculous deliverance of the man, prioritize their fear and financial loss over recognizing Jesus' power. This response is a symbolic representation of "bad soil," where the seed of the Word fails to take root.

4. **A.**
   While the man expresses a strong desire to join Jesus and follow Him, Jesus instead instructs him to stay and share his testimony with those in his own community. He's at the forefront of gentile evangelism, serving as a witness to Jesus' deliverance.

5. **B.**
   Mark describes the woman's approach as carried out "in fear and trembling" (5:33). Dr. Godfrey noted that she knew the Psalms through and through, precisely because this idea of "fear and trembling" is found in Psalm 55:5, which is what Mark is drawing on when he describes her faith.

6. **B.**
   The gospel of Mark constantly mentions eating or food. After the girl is raised, Jesus demands that someone bring her food, which marks another notable example of eating in the gospel of Mark.

9

Kingdom Healings and Opposition

INTRODUCTION

While Jesus is often portrayed as a teacher and healer cherished by all, His ministry was marked by considerable rejection and opposition. In this lesson, Dr. Godfrey explores the challenging realities surrounding Jesus' ministry, bringing to light essential truths about Christ, John the Baptist, and the opposition that comes from proclaiming the gospel.

LEARNING GOALS

When you have finished this lesson, you should be able to:

- Understand why Jesus was rejected in His hometown of Nazareth
- Explain why Jesus sent out the Apostles and how He prepared them for their mission
- Describe Herod's conflicted relationship with John the Baptist and Herod's response to the gospel

KEY IDEAS

- Jesus had a lonely ministry that was marked by misunderstanding and rejection even from those close to Him.
- God provides for those who minister His Word, even in challenging circumstances.
- The "soils" metaphor from earlier in Mark's gospel continues to illustrate the varied responses to Christ and His message.

REFLECTION & DISCUSSION QUESTIONS

Before the Video

What Do You Think?

Take a moment to answer the following questions. They will prepare you for the lecture.

- Why is the gospel so often considered offensive?

- How does the reality of rejection, even for Jesus, shape your understanding of being a Christian?

Scripture Reading

And on the Sabbath he began to teach in the synagogue, and many who heard him were astonished, saying, "Where did this man get these things? What is the wisdom given to him? How are such mighty works done by his hands? Is not this the carpenter, the son of Mary and brother of James and Joses and Judas and Simon? And are not his sisters here with us?" And they took offense at him.

—Mark 6:2–3

- Why did the people at the synagogue take offense at Jesus?

During the Video

Answer the following questions while you watch the video. They will guide you through the lecture.

Opposition to the Kingdom *0:00–13:05*

- What does Mark's recounting of Jesus' mission trip tell us about those to whom the kingdom is available?

- Why did Jesus heal the woman publicly but the little girl privately?

- Why did Jesus not do great works in Nazareth?

Herod and John the Baptist *13:05–24:57*

- How does the structure of Mark's gospel show that he is being very intentional in his placement of the account of Herod and John the Baptist?

- Why did Herod imprison John the Baptist, and how did he feel about John?

After the Video

Answer the following questions after you have finished the lecture. They will help you identify and summarize the major points.

- In what way was Jesus alone in His ministry? What does it mean that "a prophet is not without honor, except in his hometown" (Mark 6:4)?

  If you are in a group, have the members discuss how Christians should deal with feeling alone in the world. Ask: How can Christ's ministry and the church be a comfort to those who are lonely?

- Was the Apostles' mission trip successful? Why or why not? How were the Apostles to deal with rejection?

  If you are in a group, have the members discuss how Christians should handle opposition toward the gospel. Ask: How can we speak the truth in love in a hostile world?

- With what kind of interest did Herod listen to John? Did he ultimately believe John's message? Why or why not?

  If you are in a group, have some of the members describe a time when they encountered hesitancy toward the gospel because of the worldly care experienced by their hearers. Ask: What was it like? How should Christians approach those with worldly cares?

PRAYER

Commit what you have learned from God's Word in this lesson to prayer.

- Praise God for His unchanging plan of redemption, which teaches us to be steadfast even in the face of rejection and opposition.
- Confess the times when worldly rejection has discouraged you from faithfully following Christ.

- Thank God for sending messengers of His Word to bring His truth to light.
- Ask God to fill you with courage through His Spirit, allowing you to share the gospel with boldness and compassion.

REVIEW QUIZ

Use these multiple-choice questions to measure what you learned from this lesson.

1. What chiastic theme does Mark 6 begin with?
   a. Rejection
   b. Teaching
   c. Growing
   d. Calmness
2. After rejecting Jesus at Capernaum, His family finally accepts Him at Nazareth.
   a. True
   b. False
3. What was Jesus' deeper purpose in sending out the Apostles?
   a. To perform more miracles
   b. To help them learn to preach on their own
   c. To show them that God will provide
   d. To show them that the kingdom of God is here
4. Who did Herod believe that Jesus was?
   a. The King of the Jews
   b. The prophet Elijah
   c. The Messiah of God
   d. John the Baptist resurrected
5. Why was Herod's reputation on the line at his party?
   a. He wanted to please Herodias' daughter.
   b. He was at odds with the Pharisees.
   c. He had invited nobles and military officials.
   d. He needed to win the approval of his citizens.
6. What event does Mark contrast between John the Baptist and Christ?
   a. Baptism for the remission of sins
   b. Burial in a tomb
   c. Preaching in the wilderness
   d. Resurrection

Answer Key—Kingdom Healings and Opposition

REFLECTION & DISCUSSION QUESTIONS

Before the Video

What Do You Think?

These are personal questions. The answers should be based on your own knowledge and experience.

Scripture Reading

- Why did the people at the synagogue take offense at Jesus?

  The people at the synagogue were offended by Jesus because they saw Him as an ordinary person, a local carpenter, a familiar relative, and not as the long-awaited Messiah. Jesus taught in an extraordinary manner, but the people of Nazareth saw Him only as ordinary.

During the Video

Opposition to the Kingdom

- What does Mark's recounting of Jesus' mission trip tell us about those to whom the kingdom is available?

  Mark uses Christ's healing of the gentile woman and Jairus' daughter to show that all are welcome in the kingdom of God, from the greatest to the least, regardless of social standing, wealth, or background. Jairus was a prominent leader, but the woman was unclean, unnamed, and marginalized. This helps us to understand that no matter what distress someone is experiencing, Jesus welcomes all.

- Why did Jesus heal the woman publicly but the little girl privately?

  This difference emphasizes Jesus' wisdom. He operates in different ways in different circumstances. Jesus adapted to each situation, motivated not by theatrics but by His unique purpose in each miracle. In the case of Jairus' daughter, He did not want her story known.

- Why did Jesus not do great works in Nazareth?

  Jesus performed fewer miracles in Nazareth because of the people's lack of faith. It is not the case that He was unable; rather, their unbelieving hearts were the problem. Mark tells us that Jesus did lay His hands on some and heal them (6:5).

Herod and John the Baptist

- How does the structure of Mark's gospel show that he is being very intentional in his placement of the account of Herod and John the Baptist?

  The structure of Mark's gospel shows that Mark is intentional in his placement of the account of Herod and John the Baptist because it first illustrates the theme of opposition. This account foreshadows the rejection and hostility that Jesus will encounter, particularly with Herod and other authorities. Mark's arrangement is deliberate; it isn't just a sudden insertion but a thematic choice that fits into the fourth chiasm in the gospel, which emphasizes Jesus' foes.

- Why did Herod imprison John the Baptist, and how did he feel about John?

  Herod imprisoned John the Baptist for publicly condemning Herod's recent marriage to his brother's wife as unlawful. Herod, however, did have a high view of John, seeing him as a holy and righteous man.

After the Video

- In what way was Jesus alone in His ministry? What does it mean that "a prophet is not without honor, except in his hometown" (Mark 6:4)?

  Jesus had a lonely ministry because, many times, both His friends and foes failed to understand Him. As a prophet, Jesus certainly had honor and fame throughout Galilee, but in the most intimate areas of His life, He was misunderstood, despised, and rejected. By saying that "a prophet is not without honor, except in his hometown," Jesus highlighted the old adage that familiarity can breed contempt. People who had known Him from childhood were too focused on how they had previously related to Him to recognize Him for what He truly was.

- Was the Apostles' mission trip successful? Why or why not? How were the Apostles to deal with rejection?

  The Apostles' mission trip was successful, but it was also met with rejection. As Dr. Godfrey stated earlier in the series, the Word goes out for both salvation and judgment; thus, even rejection fulfills God's purpose. The Apostles dealt with rejection through the understanding that it has a negligible impact on ministry and by shaking the dust off their feet after such an occurrence.

- With what kind of interest did Herod listen to John? Did he ultimately believe John's message? Why or why not?

  Mark says that Herod "heard him gladly" (Mark 6:20), showing an interest in John's words, yet he did not act on them. Ultimately, Herod is another case of thorny soil that recognizes the Word but is too crowded by the cares of the world. He had more concern for his reputation among elites than for God's truth.

REVIEW QUIZ

1. **A.**
   Mark 6 begins with the theme of rejection, first seen in Jesus' rejection in the Gerasenes in Mark 5, but most pronounced is His rejection at Capernaum.

2. **B.**
   Even though some in Jesus' family later accept Him, they still reject Him at Nazareth, just as He was rejected at Capernaum.

3. **C.**
   Jesus' goal for the Apostles' journey was to teach them to trust in God's provision, especially in their future ministry. This is why He told them to take minimal supplies, an instruction that we might not expect for a journey. Jesus sent them out more or less as they were in order to grow their reliance on God.

4. **D.**
   Herod believed Jesus to be a resurrected John the Baptist, as Mark records (6:16). In part, this may be because, as Dr. Godfrey conjectured, Herod felt guilty for John's death at his hands.

5. **C.**
   Herod's reputation was on the line because of the presence of high-ranking guests, compelling him to uphold his rash promise to Herodias' daughter.

6. **B.**
   The burial of John by his disciples contrasts with Jesus' burial. While John's disciples were faithful to him even after his death, Jesus was buried by another, Joseph of Arimathea, because His own disciples fled.

10

The Shepherd and His Enemies

INTRODUCTION

Jesus' ministry was often misunderstood—not only by His followers and opponents, but also by His own disciples. In this lesson, Dr. Godfrey highlights key moments, including the feeding of the five thousand and Jesus' walking on water, when we see clearly that Jesus is the compassionate Shepherd, the divine "I am," and the Teacher who confronts hollow traditions with the truth of God's Word.

LEARNING GOALS

When you have finished this lesson, you should be able to:

- Identify significant occurrences of the themes of eating and bread in Jesus' ministry
- Explain the significance of Jesus' act of walking on water
- Understand and discuss the issues with the Pharisees' perspective on rituals and traditions

KEY IDEAS

- Jesus' ministry was primarily concerned with teaching and preaching over miracles.
- Jesus is the same "I am" of the Old Testament, revealing His divinity by His use of the statement and through His actions.
- Scripture is always more authoritative than the traditions of men.

REFLECTION & DISCUSSION QUESTIONS

Before the Video

What Do You Think?

Take a moment to answer the following questions. They will prepare you for the lecture.

- What might a miracle such as the feeding of the five thousand mean? What could Jesus be saying through this miracle?
- Is tradition useful for Christians? How much, if any, tradition should Christians utilize in their theology and worship?

Scripture Reading

When they saw him walking on the sea they thought it was a ghost, and cried out, for they all saw him and were terrified. But immediately he spoke to them and said, "Take heart; it is I. Do not be afraid."

—Mark 6:49–50

- Why were the disciples afraid of Jesus? What does this tell us about their trust in Him?

During the Video

Answer the following questions while you watch the video. They will guide you through the lecture.

Feeding the Sheep *0:00–9:44*

- What is the most desperate human need? How does Jesus deliver it to the crowd?
- What do the twelve baskets correspond to? What is Jesus communicating through them?

Lessons about Food *9:44–23:44*

- What does Dr. Godfrey suggest that the disciples did not understand about the loaves?

- What is a nuance of the Greek phrase for "eat" in Mark 7:3? What does it communicate?

After the Video

Answer the following questions after you have finished the lecture. They will help you identify and summarize the major points.

- What makes Jesus' meal extraordinary? What do the fish and loaves show? How does this reveal Christ as Shepherd?

  If you are in a group, have the members discuss how Christ shepherds His church now. Ask: How does Christ feed His people and provide for their needs?

- How does Jesus' walking on water parallel parts of Exodus? What does this say about His character?

  If you are in a group, have the members discuss ways that they see how the Old and New Testaments are united as one story with one God.

- What does Jesus ultimately want to be clean? How does this contrast with the Pharisaical view of cleanliness?

  If you are in a group, have the members discuss what they think are some ways to avoid a Pharisaical attitude toward God and worship. Ask: How does the heart factor into this approach?

PRAYER

Commit what you have learned from God's Word in this lesson to prayer.

- Praise God for providing your daily bread and guidance through His Word.
- Confess the times when you have failed to follow Christ, your Good Shepherd.
- Thank God for shepherding you through His Son and through His undershepherds in the church.
- Ask God for the Holy Spirit to renew your heart daily toward increasingly sincere devotion and inward purity.

REVIEW QUIZ

Use these multiple-choice questions to measure what you learned from this lesson.

1. Who should have led the “sheep without a shepherd” (Mark 6:34)?
   a. The Pharisees
   b. Herod
   c. Pilate
   d. Caiaphas
2. What quality does Jesus seek for the disciples to have when He charges them to feed the crowd?
   a. Faith
   b. Humility
   c. Responsibility
   d. Charity
3. The disciples did not encounter another storm after the feeding of the five thousand.
   a. True
   b. False
4. What recurring theme occurs during the sea encounter with Jesus?
   a. Power and authority
   b. Eating and bread
   c. Life and death
   d. Faith and fear
5. What theme is the center of Dr. Godfrey’s fourth chiasm?
   a. Miracles
   b. Tradition
   c. Enemies
   d. Feeding
6. Why did the Pharisees look down on the disciples for not washing their hands?
   a. Because of Jewish culture surrounding food
   b. Because of physical cleanliness
   c. Because of the tradition of the elders
   d. Because of Roman law

Answer Key—The Shepherd and His Enemies

REFLECTION & DISCUSSION QUESTIONS

Before the Video

What Do You Think?

These are personal questions. The answers should be based on your own knowledge and experience.

Scripture Reading

- Why were the disciples afraid of Jesus? What does this tell us about their trust in Him?

  The disciples were afraid because they mistook Jesus for a ghost, showing a lack of understanding of His divine nature. Their fear reveals a struggle of faith, but Jesus reassured them and, as this lesson will uncover, revealed the full extent of His nature through a simple phrase.

During the Video

Feeding the Sheep

- What is the most desperate human need? How does Jesus deliver it to the crowd?

  The most desperate human need is for the truth found in God's Word. Jesus responds to this need by teaching the crowd rather than focusing solely on physical feeding. His teaching is the primary means of shepherding His people.

- What do the twelve baskets correspond to? What is Jesus communicating through them?

  The twelve baskets correspond to the twelve Apostles, symbolizing that the Apostles would be equipped to spiritually nourish God's people. Through this, Jesus is preparing His Apostles for their future ministry, underscoring their own role as shepherds.

Lessons about Food

- What does Dr. Godfrey suggest that the disciples did not understand about the loaves?

  Mark says that the disciples did not understand about the loaves because they could not grasp that Jesus provides for the needs of His people, just as He also fed the five thousand. Despite seeing this amazing miracle, they remained in a state in which "their hearts were hardened" (Mark 6:52) to a degree that they could not comprehend Christ's identity and care for the crowd.

- What is a nuance of the Greek phrase for "eat" in Mark 7:3? What does it communicate?

  The Greek word for "eat" more literally means "eat bread," typically used for any meal, but the term's usage in Mark 7:3 contrasts the Pharisees' external focus on cleanliness with Jesus' teaching on the internal purity of one's heart. The Greek is meant to make us think back to all the bread that has come before in Mark's gospel—for instance, to the feeding of the five thousand. When the Pharisees talk about bread, they are talking about it only in an external way. When Jesus talks about bread, He is really talking about the internal feeding of God's people.

After the Video

- What makes Jesus' meal extraordinary? What do the fish and loaves show? How does this reveal Christ as Shepherd?

  Jesus' meal is extraordinary in its abundance and simplicity. His meal fully satisfied five thousand people, and it did so with simple foods. The fish and the loaves can be contrasted with Herod's royal delicacies, but Christ was the true Shepherd to these people by providing a meal even in the wilderness—a meal that was neither a pompous feast nor meager rations, but instead the perfect allotment of their daily bread.

- How does Jesus' walking on water parallel parts of Exodus? What does this say about His character?

  Jesus' walking on water parallels parts of Exodus in two ways. First, Jesus means to pass by His disciples (Mark 6:48), just as God passed by Moses in Exodus 33, showing just a glimpse of His glory to them. Second, Jesus says, "I am" (egō eimi), *which identifies Him as God, for God proclaimed Himself to Moses as "I AM WHO I AM" from the burning bush (Ex. 3:14). This establishes Jesus, the Son of God, as both the God of Israel and the incarnate manifestation of His glory.*

- What does Jesus ultimately want to be clean? How does this contrast with the Pharisaical view of cleanliness?

  Jesus desires the purity of the heart rather than mere external cleanliness. He ultimately wants the heart and what comes out of it to be clean. The Pharisees' view was entirely concerned with externals and the letter of the law, while Jesus rightly pointed them back to the spiritual realities that matter most to God. They should have known this from the Old Testament, since Joel declares, "Rend your hearts and not your garments" (Joel 2:13).

REVIEW QUIZ

1. **B.**
   The people should have been shepherded by Herod because he was their ruler and possessed the civic office and duty to do so. This is biblically reflected in the call of

Psalm 82 that is directed to the princes so that they might care for the weak, poor, and helpless.

2. **C.**
   Jesus seeks for the disciples to have responsibility, which is precisely why He tasks them with finding food, instead of immediately doing so Himself. For the disciples to fulfill the ministry with which Christ will entrust them, He gives them charge over the flock.

3. **A.**
   After feeding the five thousand, the disciples struggled with headwinds on the sea but were not in a full storm. Yet as Jesus had earlier calmed the storm, He calmed the wind for the disciples (Mark 6:51).

4. **D.**
   The recurring theme of faith and fear occurs in the disciples' reaction to finding Jesus walking on water. While they should be spurred to faith by this encounter, they instead lapse into fear, being terrified of Christ as if He were a ghost.

5. **B.**
   While the other themes are important to this chiasm, only the theme of tradition is at the center. The other themes proceed up and down from the focal point of tradition, making it the chiastic focus and emphasis of the passage.

6. **C.**
   The Pharisees looked down on the disciples for their eating practices because this violated the tradition of their elders, which they presumed was divine. This was not a matter of physical but rather spiritual cleanliness, according to them, and it was on par with the Mosaic law itself.

11

Traditions vs. Authority

INTRODUCTION

Tradition becomes problematic when it goes beyond Scripture. Jesus directly addressed this issue with the Pharisees, confronting them for giving priority to their traditions rather than to God's Word. In this lesson, Dr. Godfrey examines Jesus' rebuke of hypocritical traditions, the fulfillment of the Old Testament law in Christ, and His lordship in declaring all foods clean.

LEARNING GOALS

When you have finished this lesson, you should be able to:

- Understand the relationship between Scripture and tradition
- Recognize how Jesus' confrontation with the Pharisees points out the true source of what makes someone unclean
- Explain how Jesus' declaring all foods to be clean relates to the gospel

KEY IDEAS

- Scripture is the ultimate rule of faith and life.
- Jesus uses Old Testament prophecy intentionally and deliberately.
- Jesus is Lord over the Mosaic law and its fulfillment; He had the authority to end aspects of the law and declare all foods clean.

REFLECTION & DISCUSSION QUESTIONS

Before the Video

What Do You Think?

Take a moment to answer the following questions. They will prepare you for the lecture.

- Why are people sometimes more committed to traditions than to God's Word?
- How should Christians approach the Mosaic law today?

Scripture Reading

And he called the people to him again and said to them, "Hear me, all of you, and understand: There is nothing outside a person that by going into him can defile him, but the things that come out of a person are what defile him."

—Mark 7:14–15

- What do the Pharisees fundamentally get wrong in their emphasis on the traditions of the elders such as hand-washing?

During the Video

Answer the following questions while you watch the video. They will guide you through the lecture.

Acts 1 and 2 of Jesus' Confronting the Pharisees — *0:00–14:00*

- Did Jesus get angry at the Pharisees? Why or why not?
- What was Corban, and how did it circumvent the moral obligation of children to parents?

Act 3 of Jesus' Confronting the Pharisees — *14:00–24:17*

- What did Jesus say defiles a person, and what implication does Mark draw from this?

- Why did Israel have dietary laws? What was their purpose?

After the Video

Answer the following questions after you have finished the lecture. They will help you identify and summarize the major points.

- What was the essential issue with the Pharisees, and what had Isaiah prophesied about it?

  If you are in a group, ask the members to discuss the dangers of externalism. Ask: Why are people more often concerned with what others think about them than what God thinks about them?

- What example was given of the Roman Catholic Church's allowing tradition to dominate the Word of God?

  If you are in a group, have the members give examples of tradition being misused in either the church or the culture. Ask: How should Christians deal with these abuses?

- Did Jesus have the authority to declare foods clean? Why or why not? How does this fit into the Christology of Mark's gospel?

  If you are in a group, have the members discuss how Christ's authority gives comfort in an age of uncertainty. Ask: How can you further submit yourself to the loving authority of Christ?

PRAYER

Commit what you have learned from God's Word in this lesson to prayer.

- Praise God for His supreme authority over all creation.
- Confess any instances of hypocrisy in your life.
- Thank God that His Son was perfectly sincere in all that He said and did.
- Ask God to deliver you from the fear of man, that you might fear Him truly.

REVIEW QUIZ

Use these multiple-choice questions to measure what you learned from this lesson.

1. What is the primary reason that Jesus quoted from the Old Testament against the Pharisees?
   a. To score rhetorical points against them
   b. To denigrate their credibility
   c. To appeal to an external authority
   d. To provoke their knowledge of the text
2. Although the Pharisees murmured against Christ, they eventually accepted His instruction after this rebuke.
   a. True
   b. False
3. What commandment did the Pharisees violate by enforcing Corban?
   a. Sixth
   b. Ninth
   c. Fifth
   d. Fourth
4. Dr. Godfrey made a contrast between Apostolic religion and what other kind of religion?
   a. Pharisaical
   b. Extrabiblical
   c. Rabbinic
   d. Old Testament
5. Which laws of Moses still apply to Christians today?
   a. Moral
   b. Judicial
   c. Ceremonial
   d. Both a and b
6. Where did Jesus go immediately after this confrontation with the Pharisees?
   a. Jerusalem
   b. Caesarea Philippi
   c. Samaria
   d. Tyre and Sidon

Answer Key—Traditions vs. Authority

REFLECTION & DISCUSSION QUESTIONS

Before the Video

What Do You Think?

These are personal questions. The answers should be based on your own knowledge and experience.

Scripture Reading

- What do the Pharisees fundamentally get wrong in their emphasis on the traditions of the elders such as hand-washing?

  In emphasizing externals, the Pharisees have lost sight of what the traditions of the elders might have been trying to communicate about the need for internal purity. Jesus reminds them that purity of heart is what makes a person clean, not merely what is done physically and externally.

During the Video

Acts 1 and 2 of Jesus' Confronting the Pharisees

- Did Jesus get angry at the Pharisees? Why or why not?

  Yes, Jesus was angry with the Pharisees. They were self-appointed leaders who failed to be true shepherds for Israel. They were hypocrites who warranted a harsh rebuke by the true Shepherd, for they had traded the true worship of God for empty formality.

- What was Corban, and how did it circumvent the moral obligation of children to parents?

  Corban was a vow that dedicated possessions or money to God, which the Pharisees used to justify withholding financial support from one's parents. This practice contradicted the fifth commandment to honor one's father and mother by allowing a loophole that gave the appearance that one's money was being set apart for a religious purpose.

Act 3 of Jesus' Confronting the Pharisees

- What did Jesus say defiles a person, and what implication does Mark draw from this?

  Jesus explained that defilement is caused not by what a person eats but by what comes from the person's heart, such as evil thoughts and actions. Mark clarifies that this teaching implies that all foods are "clean," marking a significant shift from the Mosaic dietary laws.

- Why did Israel have dietary laws? What was their purpose?

  The dietary laws were given to Israel to separate it from the nations; these laws were for Israel's purity. They also served as a testimony to the nations that the world is partially clean and partially unclean, partially holy and partially unholy. These laws were necessary until the time came when the Holy One, the Clean One—Jesus Christ—arrived to fulfill all that the law of Moses had pointed to.

After the Video

- What was the essential issue with the Pharisees, and what had Isaiah prophesied about it?

  The essential issue with the Pharisees was their hypocrisy: they honored God outwardly but were inwardly far from Him. Their lips and heart contradicted one another. Jesus referenced this prophecy from Isaiah 29:13, but the whole chapter of Isaiah 29 is instructive regarding the Pharisees' problem and the reality of what Jesus was bringing about as the Messiah. Jesus' use of Isaiah 29 identifies the Pharisees with those who are truly against the people of Israel, as those who are blinded and stagger and have no Word from God because they do not truly fear Him (see vv. 8–13). Jesus is the ultimate fulfillment of this prophecy, for He is the One doing wonderful things among God's people, bringing about salvation, holiness, and understanding to His people (see vv. 14, 22–24).

- What example was given of the Roman Catholic Church's allowing tradition to dominate the Word of God?

  Tradition can overshadow the Word of God when it is given authority over Scripture, leading to practices that contradict biblical teachings. One example is the Roman Catholic Church's doctrine of Mary as a "mediatrix," a title formalized by the church at the Second Vatican Council. This is in conflict with Scripture, which states that Christ alone is the Mediator between God and man (1 Tim. 2:5).

- Did Jesus have the authority to declare foods clean? Why or why not? How does this fit into the Christology of Mark's gospel?

  Jesus did have the authority to declare foods clean because He was the One who had established those laws in the first place. Jesus has authority over every domain, as we've seen in Mark through His quieting storms, declaring Himself Lord of the Sabbath, and here, declaring all foods clean. We might think of food as something ordinary, but this expansion of Mark's Christology is helpful because it adds a depth and a reminder to us about Jesus' lordship: every domain of creation is subject to Him as Lord, down to the most minute details.

REVIEW QUIZ

1. **D.**
   The main reason that Jesus quoted from the Old Testament was to provoke the Pharisees' knowledge of the text. They knew the Old Testament and would immediately be aware of the condemnation that Jesus sought to pronounce against them.

2. **B.**
   The Pharisees continued to debate Jesus, and they failed to accept His instruction. Isaiah had prophesied of those who did not understand but would come to do so (Isa. 29:23–24), and Christ challenged the Pharisees to accept the truth or else they would persist in error.

3. **C.**
   The Pharisees violated the fifth commandment, which is "honor your father and your mother" (Ex. 20:12). Jesus highlighted Corban as a way that tradition was misused to sidestep direct moral obligations.

4. **C.**
   Dr. Godfrey contrasted Apostolic religion from rabbinic religion. Rabbinic religion holds fast to the Mosaic law absolutely, making the ceremonies therein eternal, while Apostolic religion points to Christ as the fulfillment of such laws.

5. **A.**
   While the whole law of Moses was good and holy, Dr. Godfrey stated that the moral law is what still applies today. The ceremonial laws prefigured Christ, and the judicial laws were a particular extension of the moral law for the nation of Israel.

6. **D.**
   Jesus went to Tyre and Sidon immediately after His confrontation with the Pharisees. Right after declaring all food clean, He went into gentile territory, to a former enemy of Israel, because through Him, all the nations of the earth would be blessed.

12

Miracles and Leaven

INTRODUCTION

Mark's gospel can be complex, filled with prophetic references, surprising miracles, and challenging teachings. Why did Jesus sometimes heal in ways that seem odd to us? And why did the disciples often struggle to understand Him? In this lesson, Dr. Godfrey recounts Jesus' healing of a deaf and mute man and His lesson to the disciples after the feeding of the four thousand.

LEARNING GOALS

When you have finished this lesson, you should be able to:

- Understand the relationship between Jesus' mission and the gentiles
- Recognize subtle allusions to the Prophets and other parts of the Old Testament
- Explain the significance of Mark's chiastic structure

KEY IDEAS

- Jesus has a deep and personal care for those He tends.
- Despite witnessing Jesus' miraculous provision, the disciples often struggled in their faith, failing to fully trust Him as the true Bread of Life.
- Faith is absolutely central to Mark's gospel.

REFLECTION & DISCUSSION QUESTIONS

Before the Video

What Do You Think?

Take a moment to answer the following questions. They will prepare you for the lecture.

- If the Jews are God's people, then why does Jesus interact with the gentiles? How does the New Testament redefine the relationship between Jews and gentiles?

- Why are there two miraculous feedings in Mark's gospel, one of five thousand and the other of four thousand? What is Mark trying to communicate through these events?

Scripture Reading

Say to those who have an anxious heart, "Be strong; fear not! Behold, your God will come with vengeance, with the recompense of God. He will come and save you." Then the eyes of the blind shall be opened, and the ears of the deaf unstopped; then shall the lame man leap like a deer, and the tongue of the mute sing for joy.

—Isaiah 35:4–6

- What does this passage tell us about Jesus' ministry?

During the Video

Answer the following questions while you watch the video. They will guide you through the lecture.

Miracles among the Gentiles *0:00–13:37*

- Explain the relationship between the woman's "crumbs" statement and the Bread of Life.

- What message might Mark have for us in reporting Jesus' command to others not to speak of His miracles but people's telling of them anyway?

Bread and Leaven *13:37–23:22*

- What objection have liberal scholars raised about the feedings of the four thousand and the five thousand? How does Dr. Godfrey respond to their objection?

- What are Dr. Godfrey's three conclusions from the disciples' reaction to the leaven?

After the Video

Answer the following questions after you have finished the lecture. They will help you identify and summarize the major points.

- Why does Jesus compare the gentiles to "dogs" when dealing with the Syrophoenician woman (Mark 7:27)?

  If you are in a group, have the members discuss why Jesus seems offensive to some. Ask: Why isn't the truth of the gospel easy?

- How does the feeding of the four thousand fit into Mark's gospel? What lesson for ministry is Jesus teaching His disciples?

  If you are in a group, have the members explain the significance of miraculous feedings in the Old and New Testaments. Ask: How are Christians spiritually nourished?

- Why is the fifth chiasm in Mark important? What is this chiasm about, and why is that significant to Mark's gospel overall?

  If you are in a group, have the members share one or more insights that they have gained from Dr. Godfrey's chiastic structures. Ask: What is helpful or confusing about thinking chiastically?

PRAYER

Commit what you have learned from God's Word in this lesson to prayer.

- Praise God for the steadfast love and mercy that He shows you daily.
- Confess the times that you have traded spiritual peace for worldly anxiety.
- Thank God for sending the true Bread of Life in His Son.
- Ask God for His Spirit to strengthen your faith.

REVIEW QUIZ

Use these multiple-choice questions to measure what you learned from this lesson.

1. Why does Mark point out that the woman was "a Syrophoenician by birth" (Mark 7:26)?
   a. To add further credibility to his gospel
   b. To emphasize that she was a gentile
   c. To simply be faithful to the story he witnessed
   d. To support the fact that Jesus was in Phoenicia
2. When healing the deaf man, how did Jesus express His sadness over the suffering of the world?
   a. He prayed to God.
   b. He embraced him.
   c. He sighed.
   d. He wept.
3. What prophecy does Jesus fulfill in healing the deaf man?
   a. Jeremiah 29
   b. Isaiah 29
   c. Jeremiah 35
   d. Isaiah 35
4. What is the lesson for ministry from the feeding of the four thousand?
   a. That we can minister to only a limited number of people
   b. That our resources diminish with increased need
   c. That whatever we give in service to Jesus will not diminish
   d. That our ministry to others will often result in hardened hearts
5. What two leavens does Jesus warn His disciples about?
   a. The leaven of the Pharisees and the Romans
   b. The leaven of the Pharisees and Herod
   c. The leaven of the Romans and Herod
   d. The leaven of the Sadducees and Herod
6. At this point in Mark, the disciples appear to be enemies of Christ.
   a. True
   b. False

Answer Key—Miracles and Leaven

REFLECTION & DISCUSSION QUESTIONS

Before the Video

What Do You Think?

These are personal questions. The answers should be based on your own knowledge and experience.

Scripture Reading

- What does this passage tell us about Jesus' ministry?

  This passage is a prophecy of what the substance of Jesus' ministry would be like. First, Jesus will give peace to those in need; second, He will save His people; and third, He will perform many miraculous healings as a part of His redemptive work.

During the Video

Miracles among the Gentiles

- Explain the relationship between the woman's "crumbs" statement and the Bread of Life.

  Even after hearing an analogy that connected gentiles to "dogs," the Syrophoenician woman's eagerness to know Christ is heard in this statement: "Even the dogs under the table eat the children's crumbs" (Mark 7:28). The woman recognizes that Jesus has primarily come for the children of Israel, but in her humility and faith, she sees that the "crumbs" from Jesus, the Bread of Life, can bring healing to her daughter, a gentile.

- What message might Mark have for us in reporting Jesus' command to others not to speak of His miracles but people's telling of them anyway?

  Despite Jesus' telling His followers to be silent after healing them, Mark continually notes how they share their testimony anyway. Mark's repetition of this pattern suggests a message for us: we shouldn't keep our mouths shut about Jesus. It is as if Mark is encouraging a talkative joy and gratitude for the gospel.

Bread and Leaven

- What objection have liberal scholars raised about the feedings of the four thousand and the five thousand? How does Dr. Godfrey respond to their objection?

  Some scholars have dismissed these miracles as mere duplications, as if there could have been only one event and the second was erroneously introduced by the

Gospel writers. Dr. Godfrey refutes this, explaining that the placement of these events within Mark's chiastic structure serves a purposeful, theological function.

- What are Dr. Godfrey's three conclusions from the disciples' reaction to the leaven?

  Dr. Godfrey concludes that the disciples are foolish for their slowness to understand, that Jesus is patient, and that we are just as slow to learn as the disciples are. Despite Jesus' continued demonstrations of His power and provision, the disciples struggle to fully trust Him, and this section of Mark's gospel concludes with Jesus' questioning them, "Do you not yet understand?" (8:21).

After the Video

- Why does Jesus compare the gentiles to "dogs" when dealing with the Syrophoenician woman (Mark 7:27)?

  Dr. Godfrey offered two reasons that Jesus compares the gentiles to dogs: First, there is truth to such a comparison, since the gentiles at this moment in redemptive history are not the children of God in the way that the Israelites are the children of God. Second, this is fundamentally a test whether the woman's faith is real or shallow. Jesus manifests the possibility of offense so that she truly approaches Him in inward faith and not just for the external benefit of healing.

- How does the feeding of the four thousand fit into Mark's gospel? What lesson for ministry is Jesus teaching His disciples?

  The feeding of the four thousand is a chiastic mirror to the feeding of the five thousand. These are two instances of feeding in a chiastic structure that help elevate the nature of God's providence and reveal Jesus as a Good Shepherd. By His example, Jesus encourages His disciples to be faithful and trusting shepherds in the future. The seven baskets from the seven loaves show that He is able to provide for their needs and that everything that they give to Him in ministry will not be diminished.

- Why is the fifth chiasm in Mark important? What is this chiasm about, and why is that significant to Mark's gospel overall?

  The fifth chiasm in Mark is important because it is the center of all its nine chiasms, and consequently, it is the focal point of Mark's gospel. This chiasm is about faith and what true faith entails, which is important because Mark's fundamental goal is to inspire faith in his audience. Even the disciples, at this point in Mark's gospel, desperately need a lesson about the nature of faith, since they do not yet have true understanding.

REVIEW QUIZ

1. **B.**

   Mark points out that the woman was a Syrophoenician by birth to further empha-

size that she was a gentile. This whole portion of Mark is highlighting the fact that Jesus' ministry extended beyond the Israelites.

2. **C.**
   When Jesus healed the deaf man, He sighed over the fallen nature of the world. While Jesus never fails to accomplish His mission, He still laments and is moved by our condition.

3. **D.**
   Jesus fulfills the prophecy found in Isaiah 35, which states, "The tongue of the mute [will] sing for joy. For waters break forth in the wilderness, and streams in the desert." This corresponds, as Dr. Godfrey noted, to Jesus' healing the man's speech, possibly hinting at the use of His spit to do so.

4. **C.**
   From the seven loaves that the disciples had, Jesus fed four thousand, and they were left with seven baskets. This is a lesson that everything that we give in service to Jesus will not diminish what we have; even if it appears so temporally, it will not ultimately be the case.

5. **B.**
   Jesus warns His disciples about the leaven of the Pharisees and the leaven of Herod. The former represents established religion and the latter represents civil government, both of which were corrupting spiritual influences at the time.

6. **A.**
   This section of Mark ends with the question, "Do you not yet understand?" (8:21). The disciples' misunderstanding of Jesus' teachings and failure to recognize Him appear to put them at odds with Him in this section about Jesus' enemies.

13

Teaching True Faith

INTRODUCTION

The gospel of Mark is structured in such a way that the subject of faith is at its center. Faith in Christ is transformative, and Mark highlights the transformation of the disciples as they are challenged and built up by Christ to have a faith that will endure what is soon to come in His earthly ministry. In this lesson, Dr. Godfrey guides us through the structure and text of Mark's narrative to explain essential truths about faith, suffering, and discipleship.

LEARNING GOALS

When you have finished this lesson, you should be able to:

- Explain the significance of Jesus' healing the blind
- Understand the meaning and implications of taking up one's cross
- Contrast the disciples' perception of Jesus' mission with His teaching on suffering and glory

KEY IDEAS

- The disciples demonstrate an incomplete faith in Christ.
- True faith encompasses trust in both Jesus and His Word.
- Christian suffering precedes Christian glory.

REFLECTION & DISCUSSION QUESTIONS

Before the Video

What Do You Think?

Take a moment to answer the following questions. They will prepare you for the lecture.

- What is the difference between a simple, temporary faith and a true, lasting faith?

- Why do Christians experience suffering on account of their faith, and what is the appropriate response to such suffering?

Scripture Reading

> *"If anyone would come after me, let him deny himself and take up his cross and follow me. For whoever would save his life will lose it, but whoever loses his life for my sake and the gospel's will save it. For what does it profit a man to gain the whole world and forfeit his soul?"*
>
> —Mark 8:34–36

- What actions reflect the life of a true believer?

During the Video

Answer the following questions while you watch the video. They will guide you through the lecture.

True Faith *0:00–13:44*

- What did Jesus teach His disciples privately, and did they grasp His meaning?

- Who was Jesus rumored to be, and who recognized His true identity?

A Kingdom of Suffering *13:44–24:03*

- Why does Jesus tell Peter, "Get behind me, Satan!" (Mark 8:33)?

- Why is the expression "take up his cross" (Mark 8:34) so radical? How would this have struck Jesus' hearers?

- What criticism do liberal theologians level against Jesus' prophecy that "there are some standing here who will not taste death until they see the kingdom of God after it has come with power" (Mark 9:1)? Why is this criticism unfounded?

After the Video

Answer the following questions after you have finished the lecture. They will help you identify and summarize the major points.

- Why does Jesus heal the blind man from Bethsaida in two stages? What do the stages represent?

  If you are in a group, have the members discuss parts of Scripture that they might find confusing. Ask: Rather than distance us from understanding Scripture, how can difficult texts bring us closer to God?

- What principle do we discover in Jesus' prophecy of His suffering and death?

  If you are in a group, have the members provide examples that show the importance of suffering in Christian life. Ask: How does suffering unite us further to Christ?

- Why does Jesus emphasize not being ashamed of both Himself and His words? Why might He have added "and of my words" (Mark 8:38)?

  If you are in a group, have the members give a sense of how they understand Christ's teaching—if they find Him hard to understand or clear, for example. Ask: Why should we obey the words of Christ even when it is costly?

PRAYER

Commit what you have learned from God's Word in this lesson to prayer.

- Praise God for His willingness to send His Son to suffer and die on our behalf.
- Confess ways that you are tempted to seek glory apart from suffering.
- Thank God for the Holy Spirit, who opened your eyes and gave you spiritual sight.
- Ask God for strength to take up your cross and follow Jesus wholeheartedly.

REVIEW QUIZ

Use these multiple-choice questions to measure what you learned from this lesson.

1. Why didn't the disciples ask Jesus for clarity when they did not understand Him?
    a. Because they had no desire to know
    b. Because they were unsure whether He was the Messiah
    c. Because they saw Him as a mere man
    d. Because they were afraid
2. Some Old Testament prophets healed the blind as a type of the coming Christ.
    a. True
    b. False
3. According to Dr. Godfrey, the path of Christianity is a path of what?
    a. Self-denial
    b. Faith
    c. Teaching
    d. Loneliness
4. Why is it never profitable for a man to gain the whole world?
    a. It is a vain endeavor.
    b. It denies the value of the soul.
    c. It is an occasion for human evil.
    d. All of the above.
5. After suffering, where does the glory for believers come from?
    a. From the fruit of the Christian life
    b. From the Holy Spirit's witness in their hearts
    c. From the Son of Man's return with His angels
    d. From the millennial kingdom of God when it comes on earth
6. How is it true that some who heard Christ also saw the kingdom of God coming with power?
    a. They witnessed it figuratively through their descendants.
    b. They witnessed it in their hearts.
    c. They witnessed the transfiguration.
    d. They witnessed the destruction of the temple.

Answer Key—Teaching True Faith

REFLECTION & DISCUSSION QUESTIONS

Before the Video

What Do You Think?

These are personal questions. The answers should be based on your own knowledge and experience.

Scripture Reading

- What actions reflect the life of a true believer?

  Jesus commands all those who would truly come after Him to deny themselves and live entirely for Him. Paul expresses this life when he states, "It is no longer I who live, but Christ who lives in me" (Gal. 2:20). This is not something we do in our own strength but something for which we rely on Christ, especially in our cross bearing.

During the Video

True Faith

- What did Jesus teach His disciples privately, and did they grasp His meaning?

  Jesus secretly taught the disciples about His coming death and resurrection in Jerusalem. This is the first mention of this teaching in Mark's gospel, and it explicitly confirms what Jesus' ministry has been leading up to, even though His hour had not yet come. Although the disciples heard Jesus, they were unable to understand what He meant, and they were fearful, which Mark regularly contrasts with having faith.

- Who was Jesus rumored to be, and who recognized His true identity?

  Jesus was rumored to be many different things, with some calling Him a prophet and even Elijah or John the Baptist. But Peter, representing the disciples, rightly confessed that Jesus is the Christ and the true Messiah, which is significant because Peter, as Dr. Godfrey says, typically "gets every question wrong."

A Kingdom of Suffering

- Why does Jesus tell Peter, "Get behind me, Satan!" (Mark 8:33)?

  Jesus rebukes Peter because Peter rebuked Him! Mark tells us that Peter "began" to rebuke Jesus, as if it were a sustained rebuke. Peter had a notion of the Messiah that was all triumph without suffering. Jesus' calling Peter "Satan" reminds us of the wilderness temptation, in which, as other gospels record, Satan tempted Jesus with all the kingdoms of this world without a cross.

- Why is the expression "take up his cross" (Mark 8:34) so radical? How would this have struck Jesus' hearers?

  The reference to taking up one's cross is radical because one took up the cross right before the shameful execution of crucifixion. This phrase would have struck Jesus' hearers as very peculiar, symbolizing extreme self-denial and a willingness to face death.

- What criticism do liberal theologians level against Jesus' prophecy that "there are some standing here who will not taste death until they see the kingdom of God after it has come with power" (Mark 9:1)? Why is this criticism unfounded?

  Some claim that Jesus wrongly predicted His imminent return, interpreting His words as a failed prophecy. But Dr. Godfrey clarifies that Jesus' statement refers to the transfiguration and the unfolding of His kingdom's power, not a failed prediction of the second coming.

After the Video

- Why does Jesus heal the blind man from Bethsaida in two stages? What do the stages represent?

  Dr. Godfrey suggested that Jesus heals the blind man in two parts to hint at a deeper truth beyond what occurred. Just as the man sees only partially after the first stage in the healing, so too do the disciples and many of Jesus' followers see Him only partially at this point in Mark's gospel. This healing sets the stage for Jesus to finally heal the disciples of their spiritual blindness, further setting the stage for the theme of faith.

- What principle do we discover in Jesus' prophecy of His suffering and death?

  We discover what Dr. Godfrey called "the pattern of Christianity," that suffering precedes glory, that humiliation precedes exaltation. Jesus' prophecy about His suffering and death teaches the disciples about the order of suffering in the Christian life. Jesus taught this to His disciples in His earlier lessons about rejection, and He is now about to demonstrate this in full through His death and resurrection, ultimately setting the archetype for the Christian life of service and suffering.

- Why does Jesus emphasize not being ashamed of both Himself and His words? Why might He have added "and of my words" (Mark 8:38)?

  Jesus says that one must not be ashamed of both His person and His words so that people accept Him as He truly is. It is easy to invent fictitious ideas about who Jesus is, just as Peter did, and so He says this to fully secure that one must have a complete, Christ-informed faith in Him. Dr. Godfrey suggested that this message parallels Peter's confusion about Jesus; Peter was not ashamed of Jesus' being the Messiah, but was ashamed of the idea of His suffering and dying. Here, Jesus reveals that faith in Him is full and total, and not just partial sight, as the blind man had in the first stage of his healing.

REVIEW QUIZ

1. **D.**
   The disciples did not ask Jesus what He meant concerning His death and resurrection because they were afraid to do so. Dr. Godfrey observed that Mark records this to point back to the relationship between faith and fear, showing that the disciples were still ultimately fearful.

2. **B.**
   Although Isaiah had prophesied about the healing of the blind by the Messiah (Isa. 42:7), no one healed the blind in his time or earlier, making this a unique feature of Jesus' ministry and the New Testament.

3. **A.**
   Dr. Godfrey stated, "The path of Christianity is a path of self-denial." Christianity is about dying to self and living to God. As Paul says in Galatians, "It is no longer I who live, but Christ who lives in me" (Gal. 2:20).

4. **D.**
   It is not truly profitable for a man to gain the world because it is vain, not worth his soul, and evil. The soul has eternal value and is worth more than anything the world can offer, and historically, grasping for human glory has often led to horrible suffering.

5. **C.**
   Although believers are ultimately vindicated, this is not fully so until the Son of Man returns with His angels. Even though believers are freed from suffering at death, the fullness of glory is still yet to come. Revelation speaks of the saints in heaven waiting for such glory (Rev. 6:10), and that will be the case for all Christians until Jesus consummates the kingdom.

6. **C.**
   Some of Jesus' disciples saw the kingdom of God coming with power because He was transfigured before their eyes. Matthew, Mark, and Luke all put the transfiguration immediately after this statement to highlight that the transfiguration is part of Christ's inauguration of the kingdom and a glimpse of His glory.

14

The Beloved Son and a Distressed Father

INTRODUCTION

The glory of the Son of God was glimpsed in the transfiguration, and He was again declared by the Father to be "my beloved Son" (Mark 9:7). In this lesson, Dr. Godfrey explores how the transfiguration of Christ reveals His glory, His fulfillment of the Old Testament, and His relationship to suffering and glory. The disciples, despite seeing His glory, were slow to understand and unable to cast out a demon that had possessed a child of a distressed father who had come to them for help.

LEARNING GOALS

When you have finished this lesson, you should be able to:

- Understand the theological significance of the transfiguration
- Identify the themes of suffering and glory in the transfiguration
- Explain the intensity of demonic activity in the Gospels

KEY IDEAS

- Christ fulfills the entirety of the Old Testament, as embodied by Moses and Elijah in His transfiguration.
- The themes of death, resurrection, and discipleship frame the central message of the gospel of Mark.
- The main opposition to Christianity was during the life of Christ.

REFLECTION & DISCUSSION QUESTIONS

Before the Video

What Do You Think?

Take a moment to answer the following questions. They will prepare you for the lecture.

- Who is Jesus?
- Why does Jesus encounter so many demons during His ministry? How does He interact with them?

Scripture Reading

And they asked him, "Why do the scribes say that first Elijah must come?" And he said to them, "Elijah does come first to restore all things. And how is it written of the Son of Man that he should suffer many things and be treated with contempt? But I tell you that Elijah has come, and they did to him whatever they pleased, as it is written of him."

—Mark 9:11–13

- Who might be the Elijah that has come? What is his relationship to the Son of Man?

During the Video

Answer the following questions while you watch the video. They will guide you through the lecture.

The Transfiguration *0:00–11:57*

- Why were Jesus' clothes changed, and why does Mark focus on them?
- What does Peter say is more reliable than eyewitness testimony? How does this relate to the transfiguration?
- What does Jesus instruct His disciples after the transfiguration, and what might this signify?

Children and Fathers *11:57–24:27*

- What theme surrounds the center of this lesson's chiasm? When does this theme first occur?

- Where is Mark's focus in his telling of Jesus' healing of the demon-possessed boy?

After the Video

Answer the following questions after you have finished the lecture. They will help you identify and summarize the major points.

- What is the significance of Moses' and Elijah's appearing alongside Jesus? What does it say about Jesus?

  If you are in a group, ask the members how the transfiguration demonstrates the relationship of the New Testament to the Old.

- What was Elijah's role as prophesied in Malachi? What would he do? How was this fulfilled?

  If you are in a group, have the members explain why the earlier prophets are significant to Jesus' ministry.

- Why did Jesus have to deal with so much demonic activity?

  If you are in a group, have the members discuss spiritual warfare. Ask: How does Jesus' power over demons inform how we face spiritual warfare, whether it be between the world, the flesh, or the devil?

PRAYER

Commit what you have learned from God's Word in this lesson to prayer.

- Praise God for His divine glory, as the One "who dwells in unapproachable light" (1 Tim. 6:16).
- Confess the times that you have been reluctant, on account of your sin, to approach God in Christ, though He gives you access to Him through Christ.

- Thank God for revealing His glory to us in the person of Christ.
- Ask God to more fully conform you to the image of His Son through the Spirit, so that your life more fully reflects Christ's glory.

REVIEW QUIZ

Use these multiple-choice questions to measure what you learned from this lesson.

1. What psalm might Mark be alluding to in his description of Jesus' clothes during the transfiguration?
   a. Psalm 103
   b. Psalm 104
   c. Psalm 105
   d. Psalm 106
2. What reason does Mark give for Peter's suggestion of pitching tents for Jesus, Moses, and Elijah?
   a. He was overjoyed.
   b. He was nervous.
   c. He was excited.
   d. He was terrified.
3. Where does Peter later reference the transfiguration?
   a. Mark
   b. Acts
   c. 1 Peter
   d. 2 Peter
4. At this point in Mark's gospel, the disciples believed in the resurrection of the dead.
   a. True
   b. False
5. Which gospel has the most detailed account of the man and his possessed son?
   a. Matthew
   b. Mark
   c. Luke
   d. John
6. When does the New Testament begin reporting less about the activity of evil spirits?
   a. Luke
   b. John
   c. Acts
   d. Hebrews

Answer Key—The Beloved Son and a Distressed Father

REFLECTION & DISCUSSION QUESTIONS

Before the Video

What Do You Think?

These are personal questions. The answers should be based on your own knowledge and experience.

Scripture Reading

- Who might be the Elijah that has come? What is his relationship to the Son of Man?

  The Elijah that has come is John the Baptist (see Matt. 11:13–14), and he experienced the same type of persecution that Jesus would face, suffering and dying and thus foreshadowing Christ's ministerial work.

During the Video

The Transfiguration

- Why were Jesus' clothes changed, and why does Mark focus on them?

  Jesus' clothes were changed in the transfiguration as a glimpse of His divine glory. Mark emphasizes this detail because it was extraordinary. As a carpenter, Jesus would have ordinarily had very common clothing, but now the disciples who were present saw Him with the radiance of the Son of God.

- What does Peter say is more reliable than eyewitness testimony? How does this relate to the transfiguration?

  In his second epistle, Peter says: "We were eyewitnesses of his majesty. For when he received honor and glory from God the Father, and the voice was borne to him by the Majestic Glory, 'This is my beloved Son, with whom I am well pleased,' we ourselves heard this very voice borne from heaven, for we were with him on the holy mountain. And we have the prophetic word more fully confirmed" (2 Peter 1:16–19). Dr. Godfrey holds to an interpretation that Peter is teaching that God's Word is even more sure than his experience of the transfiguration.

- What does Jesus instruct His disciples after the transfiguration, and what might this signify?

  As they descend the mountain, Jesus commands His disciples to keep silent about what they saw in the transfiguration. This reinforces the pattern of suffering before glory; the disciples must grasp the necessity of Jesus' coming death and resurrection before proclaiming His glory.

Children and Fathers

- What theme surrounds the center of this lesson's chiasm? When does this theme first occur?

  The theme at the center of this chiasm about faith is Jesus' foretelling His death and resurrection, which is surrounded by the theme of children. This chiastic theme is first introduced in relation to Jesus' statement about Elijah. After Jesus' prophecy of death and resurrection, the theme of children is made even more explicit with the story of a man who approaches Christ and His disciples because he wants deliverance for his son.

- Where is Mark's focus in his telling of Jesus' healing of the demon-possessed boy?

  The Synoptic Gospels each emphasize a different aspect of Jesus' healing. Mark focuses less on the disciples or on Jesus and, with much greater detail, focuses more closely on the father of the boy.

After the Video

- What is the significance of Moses' and Elijah's appearing alongside Jesus? What does it say about Jesus?

  Moses and Elijah are significant in the transfiguration because of what they implicitly reveal. Since Moses is the key figure of the Law and Elijah is the same for the Prophets, they show that Jesus is the complete fulfillment of the Old Testament. Furthermore, this reveals more about the resurrection. Not only do those who die still live (Matt. 22:32), but they are alive in and with Christ, who is the resurrection Himself (John 11:25).

- What was Elijah's role as prophesied in Malachi? What would he do? How was this fulfilled?

  Elijah, as Malachi states, is intended to be the Messiah's forerunner, and Mark connects Malachi's prophecy with a prophecy of Isaiah in the book's prologue (Mark 1:2). After the transfiguration, Jesus states that Elijah has indeed come. One significant reason for his coming was to "turn the hearts of fathers to their children and the hearts of children to their fathers" (Mal. 4:6). His coming brought a restoration to the truth. John the Baptist fulfilled this role, preparing the way for Jesus by calling for repentance.

- Why did Jesus have to deal with so much demonic activity?

  Although the amount of demonic activity in the Gospels can seem strange given our everyday experience, the demonic presence and opposition to Jesus is perfectly reasonable. Satan and his workers were the main opposition to Christ. Because

Jesus came to bind the "strong man" (Mark 3:27), it is natural that the strong man would send all his resources to stop Jesus, which is why we see so much demonic activity in the Gospels.

REVIEW QUIZ

1. **B.**
   In describing Jesus' clothes during the transfiguration, Mark might be subtly alluding to Psalm 104, which says, "You are clothed with splendor and majesty, covering yourself with light as with a garment" (vv. 1–2).

2. **D.**
   Concerning Peter's suggestion, Mark recounts that "he did not know what to say, for they were terrified" (9:6). Peter did, however, recognize the glory of the occasion and naturally wanted to extend their experience of it.

3. **D.**
   Peter later references the transfiguration in 2 Peter, where he writes, "We were eyewitnesses of his majesty" (1:16).

4. **A.**
   Although they did not understand the meaning of it (see Mark 9:10), the disciples did believe in the resurrection, which was typical of most Jews at that time (except the Sadducees). Their problem was that they still could not grasp that Christ's death and resurrection were necessary and thought of the resurrection only in reference to the last day.

5. **B.**
   Mark, surprisingly, has the most detailed account of this healing. Because Mark is by far the shortest gospel, this draws the reader to pay extra attention to the content of this part of the narrative because Mark is expanding on it with intent to emphasize it.

6. **C.**
   The New Testament starts mentioning less about the activity of evil spirits in the book of Acts. Acts does record demonic activity, but not with the same frequency as the Gospels.

15

The Powerful Weakness of Faith

INTRODUCTION

As Jesus continues to set His face toward Jerusalem, He teaches His disciples more about the true nature of faith—its humility, dependence, and power. Faith, though it admits of our weakness, is powerful. In this lesson, Dr. Godfrey helps explain the center of Mark's gospel, examining the irony of our being weak, yet having a powerful faith.

LEARNING GOALS

When you have finished this lesson, you should be able to:

- Explain why the Apostles had authority, yet struggled over the demonic
- Describe Mark's teaching on strong and genuine faith
- Understand what true greatness in the kingdom entails

KEY IDEAS

- Faith is powerful because of the power and authority of Christ.
- It is not in greatness that the kingdom will go forward but in weakness.
- Children are a vital part of the kingdom of God.

REFLECTION & DISCUSSION QUESTIONS

Before the Video

What Do You Think?

Take a moment to answer the following questions. They will prepare you for the lecture.

- Why is faith powerful?

- What might cause someone to struggle with faith, even when the person has seen God's work in his or her life?

Scripture Reading

For he was teaching his disciples, saying to them, "The Son of Man is going to be delivered into the hands of men, and they will kill him. And when he is killed, after three days he will rise." But they did not understand the saying, and were afraid to ask him.

—Mark 9:31–32

- Why do you think the disciples were afraid of Jesus' prophecy?

During the Video

Answer the following questions while you watch the video. They will guide you through the lecture.

The Call to Faith *0:00–14:03*

- Who is the "faithless generation" that Jesus speaks of (Mark 9:19)? Why did He say this to them?

- Is the father's faith perfect? How does he react to Jesus' call to believe?

Greatness in the Kingdom *14:03–24:07*

- Did the disciples properly understand suffering and glory? Why or why not?

- What does Jesus use to teach the principle that the kingdom will go forward not in greatness but in weakness?

After the Video

Answer the following questions after you have finished the lecture. They will help you identify and summarize the major points.

- What is the Pentecostal reading of the nature of faith in the interaction between Jesus and the father? What alternative reading did Dr. Godfrey propose? Why?

  If you are in a group, have the members discuss ways in which they interpret faith as if it were a work. Ask: What are ways that we can avoid mistaking the nature of faith?

- Why couldn't the disciples cast the evil spirit out, according to Jesus?

  If you are in a group, have the members explain how Christians today should approach the spiritual realm. Ask: What is important to remember in discussions about angels and demons?

- What is the central prophecy of this section? How does it relate to the boy and his father? Why is it central?

  If you are in a group, have the members discuss Dr. Godfrey's chiastic structure. Ask: What have you learned about Mark that you did not expect?

PRAYER

Commit what you have learned from God's Word in this lesson to prayer.

- Praise God for His kind and fatherly love.
- Confess any unbelief that prevails over your faith in Christ.
- Thank God for bestowing His grace on all kinds of people, from the greatest to the least.
- Ask God to give you a strong faith in weakness through His Spirit.

REVIEW QUIZ

Use these multiple-choice questions to measure what you learned from this lesson.

1. What did Dr. Godfrey suggest is a better translation for "they were not able" (Mark 9:18)?
   a. "They were not faithful."
   b. "They were too weak."
   c. "They were not strong enough."
   d. "They were too fearful."
2. The father distrusts Jesus after His disciples were unable to heal his son.
   a. True
   b. False
3. Why are all things possible for one who believes?
   a. Our faith is infinitely powerful.
   b. God rewards faith with all things.
   c. Faith is the highest virtue.
   d. Faith trusts in Christ.
4. Why did people claim that the boy died after his exorcism?
   a. Because Jesus resurrected him
   b. Because the demon killed him
   c. Because he looked like a corpse
   d. Both a and b
5. Why is it strange that Jesus spoke of the least as the greatest?
   a. Because Jesus was the greatest
   b. Because servants did not partake at the royal banquets
   c. Because the least in society were never given royal honor
   d. Because Greco-Roman kings would have servants at their tables
6. Of which person did Jesus say that if we receive him or her, we are truly receiving Him?
   a. Disciple
   b. Child
   c. Orphan
   d. Widow

Answer Key—The Powerful Weakness of Faith

REFLECTION & DISCUSSION QUESTIONS

Before the Video

What Do You Think?

These are personal questions. The answers should be based on your own knowledge and experience.

Scripture Reading

- Why do you think the disciples were afraid of Jesus' prophecy?

  The disciples were afraid of Jesus' prophecy because it spoke of His being killed. This would have gone against their expectations of the Messiah and their expectations of greatness as His followers. In this lesson, Dr. Godfrey identifies their fear as an element of their hardness of heart.

During the Video

The Call to Faith

- Who is the "faithless generation" that Jesus speaks of (Mark 9:19)? Why did He say this to them?

  Jesus called the disciples the "faithless generation" because the disciples were unable to cast out the boy's demon as a result of their unbelief.

- Is the father's faith perfect? How does he react to Jesus' call to believe?

  The father's faith is ultimately imperfect, which is why he cries, "I believe; help my unbelief!" (Mark 9:24). Yet when Jesus calls him to faith, he puts a firm trust in Him, despite the weakness of the flesh. The father has faith but recognizes that he must trust Christ even with his faithlessness.

Greatness in the Kingdom

- Did the disciples properly understand suffering and glory? Why or why not?

  The disciples did not properly understand suffering and glory, even after Jesus' prophecy of His death and resurrection. This is because they were still concerned with worldly affairs and who had the glory among them at that time, instead of with the glory to come (Mark 9:34). At this point in Mark's gospel, they may have believed in part, but plenty of unbelief was still triumphing in their thoughts and actions.

- What does Jesus use to teach the principle that the kingdom will go forward not in greatness but in weakness?

  Jesus uses children to teach this lesson to His disciples. After healing a child with an unclean spirit, He "took a child and put him in the midst of them, and taking him in his arms, he said to them, 'Whoever receives one such child in my name receives me, and whoever receives me, receives not me but him who sent me'" (Mark 9:36–37). Dr. Godfrey paraphrases this as follows: "My kingdom is like this child, a child who is not powerful, doesn't have strength in himself, but My kingdom is like becoming a child."

After the Video

- What is the Pentecostal reading of the nature of faith in the interaction between Jesus and the father? What alternative reading did Dr. Godfrey propose? Why?

  The Pentecostal reading of Mark 9 holds that Jesus told the man "If you can" (Mark 9:23) to effectively say: "It isn't whether I can; it is whether you can. Do you have enough faith?" (Dr. Godfrey's paraphrase of the view). This reading of the text is implausible, because Jesus appears to be quoting the man's assertion ("if you can") back to him. Because of this, Dr. Godfrey suggested that the true meaning of the text is Jesus' challenging the father's doubt and furthermore hinting at the fact that He is the absolutely omnipotent Son of God.

- Why couldn't the disciples cast the evil spirit out, according to Jesus?

  The disciples were unable to cast out the demon because of lack of faith. This is why Jesus tells them that "this kind cannot be driven out by anything but prayer" (Mark 9:29); they needed to trust God in prayer to cast the demon out. Jesus is not reducing exorcism down to a rote prayer; rather, He is showing that trust in God through prayer is necessary. To testify to this point, the sons of Sceva tried to use Christ's name without true faith, and thus they were overpowered by the evil spirit (Acts 19:13–16).

- What is the central prophecy of this section? How does it relate to the boy and his father? Why is it central?

  The central prophecy of this section is Jesus' foretelling of His death and resurrection (Mark 9:30–32). He had already spoken of this at the Mount of Transfiguration (vv. 9–10), but now He plainly speaks about it to all His disciples. Jesus' prophecy of His death and resurrection parallels the previous anecdote because of the boy's apparent "death" and revival. This event, which Dr. Godfrey called a "mini-resurrection," foreshadows the fullness of the resurrection found in Christ and further points to the centrality of the resurrection in the gospel of Mark.

REVIEW QUIZ

1. **C.**
   *Dr. Godfrey suggested that the verse instead be translated "they were not strong enough" (Mark 9:18). This is because it is more consistent with the Greek text, which speaks of strength (*ischyō*—attributed to the disciples) and not about ability in a more general sense (*dynamai*—later attributed to Jesus).*

2. **A.**
   The father does distrust Jesus, since he asks, "If you can do anything . . ." (Mark 9:22). He originally had hope that his son could be saved, but after the disciples demonstrated a lack of strength, now he doubts whether anyone will help his son.

3. **D.**
   All things are possible for one who believes, precisely because the person believes in Christ as the object of his or her faith. We do not rely on the quality of our faith, but we look to Christ as the object of our faith and rely on His strength.

4. **C.**
   Those who were around him claimed that the boy with the demon had died because he looked "like a corpse" after the exorcism (Mark 9:26). Although Jesus did resurrect people during His ministry, He never allowed demons to kill them, nor did this child die; he was fully delivered by Christ.

5. **B.**
   The idea that the least is the greatest is odd because the whole point of being the king's greatest man was to sit at the banquet table and have servants waiting on you. This reversal of roles seems counterintuitive, but it is really fundamental to the Christian message of humility before exaltation and death before resurrection.

6. **B.**
   Jesus said, "Whoever receives one such child in my name receives me" (Mark 9:37). Jesus received children because the kingdom of God belongs to them (10:14) but also to show what posture the disciples must adopt to follow Christ.

16

The Call to Self-Denial

INTRODUCTION

Christianity offers the promise of glory and life in God's kingdom, but as the gospel of Mark often teaches, suffering and self-denial come before this glory. But what is the purpose of self-denial? And why did Jesus insist on it? In this lesson, Dr. Godfrey explores the concept of self-denial in multiple spheres of life, echoing Jesus' call for all to join Him in self-denial.

LEARNING GOALS

When you have finished this lesson, you should be able to:

- Understand the connection between the gospel and offense
- Explain why Jesus was so emphatic about self-denial
- Articulate the essence of marriage and issues surrounding divorce

KEY IDEAS

- Christians should avoid imposing extra burdens or obligations on others.
- Self-denial is an essential aspect of following Jesus.
- Divorce, while sometimes permitted, falls short of God's design for marriage.

REFLECTION & DISCUSSION QUESTIONS

Before the Video

What Do You Think?

Take a moment to answer the following questions. They will prepare you for the lecture.

- What does it mean to deny oneself? How are Christians to practice self-denial?

- What do you understand about the New Testament's teaching on hell? What did Jesus teach about hell?

Scripture Reading

John said to him, "Teacher, we saw someone casting out demons in your name, and we tried to stop him, because he was not following us." But Jesus said, "Do not stop him, for no one who does a mighty work in my name will be able soon afterward to speak evil of me. For the one who is not against us is for us."

—Mark 9:38–40

- Why does Jesus support those who are not opposed to Him?

During the Video

Answer the following questions while you watch the video. They will guide you through the lecture.

Sacrificing the Self — *0:00–12:55*

- Why did the disciples try to stop others from casting out demons, and why is this ironic?

- Why does Jesus use extreme language about cutting off body parts in self-denial? Should these statements be understood literally?

Marriage and Divorce — *12:55–24:20*

- Is Jesus' teaching on divorce randomly placed in Mark's narrative? Why or why not?

- What does divorce have to do with self-denial?

After the Video

Answer the following questions after you have finished the lecture. They will help you identify and summarize the major points.

- What does Jesus mean by speaking of a millstone? Which Scripture passage does this allude to, and what implications does this teaching have?

  If you are in a group, have the members explain the difference between offense at the gospel and offense at human teaching. Ask: Why is this difference important?

- How do Christ's miracles allude to the call to self-denial? Why is self-denial important?

  If you are in a group, have a few of the members share a time or trial that required self-denial. Ask: How should we continue to foster self-denial?

- What was the prevailing Jewish teaching on divorce in Jesus' time, and how did He respond?

  If you are in a group, have the members discuss how Christians can cultivate godly marriages. Ask: What passages of Scripture would be helpful here?

PRAYER

Commit what you have learned from God's Word in this lesson to prayer.

- Praise God for Christ's example of self-denial.
- Confess any tendencies toward selfishness and lack of self-denial.
- Thank God for His sanctifying work in us to make us living sacrifices.
- Ask God to embolden you toward a life of self-denial in His Spirit.

REVIEW QUIZ

Use these multiple-choice questions to measure what you learned from this lesson.

1. What does Jesus essentially tell the disciples to do to the strangers in Mark 9:38–41?
   a. Encourage them
   b. Question them
   c. Join them
   d. Rebuke them
2. Who did Dr. Godfrey say that the "little ones" are in Mark 9:42?
   a. Children only
   b. Children and new believers
   c. Children and parents
   d. Children and strangers
3. Who has the most explicit teaching about hell in the New Testament?
   a. Paul
   b. Peter
   c. Luke
   d. Jesus
4. What explanation was given for Jesus' telling the disciples to have "salt in yourselves" (Mark 9:50)?
   a. Salt signified holiness.
   b. Salt signified acceptability.
   c. Salt signified wealth.
   d. Salt signified divine life.
5. What did Dr. Godfrey propose is the reason that the Pharisees questioned Jesus about divorce?
   a. There was no set teaching on divorce.
   b. Many Pharisees had been divorced.
   c. They thought He would be strict.
   d. Divorce was inherently controversial.
6. Biblically, there can never be divorce.
   a. True
   b. False

Answer Key—The Call to Self-Denial

REFLECTION & DISCUSSION QUESTIONS

Before the Video

What Do You Think?

These are personal questions. The answers should be based on your own knowledge and experience.

Scripture Reading

- Why does Jesus support those who are not opposed to Him?

  Jesus endorses those who are not against Him because only true believers are for Him. Since these unnamed people trust in the true Christ and follow His teaching, they are not to be rebuked but commended.

During the Video

Sacrificing the Self

- Why did the disciples try to stop others from casting out demons, and why is this ironic?

  The disciples tried to stop others from casting out demons because they were not part of Jesus' core group. This is ironic because, though the disciples were closely associated with Jesus, these other men were successfully casting out demons through trust in Christ; the disciples could not previously do so. This shows that they were concerned more about their status, that others would follow them, than they were about following Jesus.

- Why does Jesus use extreme language about cutting off body parts in self-denial? Should these statements be understood literally?

  Jesus uses extreme language to teach people the theme of self-denial. This is hyperbole, which states something in extreme language to emphasize an underlying point. Because of this, Christians do not need to literally cut off limbs, but rather, in line with the historical interpretation of this text, they ought to deny themselves spiritually.

Marriage and Divorce

- Is Jesus' teaching on divorce randomly placed in Mark's narrative? Why or why not?

  Jesus' teaching on divorce with the Pharisees seems to be out of place at first sight, but it is perfectly situated in the context. Before this, Jesus talked about children, and after this, He once again mentions children, which are the fruit of marriage. Mark is crafting a picture of the kingdom's character, what it means for marriage, and the role of children and strangers in it.

- What does divorce have to do with self-denial?

  Divorce in the first-century Jewish context was often initiated for selfish reasons. In these marriages, there was a lack of self-denial, but stable marriages come from self-denial. This is why Paul uses Christ as an example of self-denial for husbands to follow; he writes, "Husbands, love your wives, as Christ loved the church and gave himself up for her" (Eph. 5:25).

After the Video

- What does Jesus mean by speaking of a millstone? Which Scripture passage does this allude to, and what implications does this teaching have?

  When Jesus speaks of a millstone, He is subtly hinting at the idea of offense, specifically the "stone of offense" found in Isaiah 8:14. This is important because it tells us that the only thing worth stumbling over is the truth of Christ, and that Christians ought not to create other requirements or demands that people might stumble over. This is why Peter rightfully calls Christ the "rock of offense" (1 Peter 2:8), since here, Christ is showing that He alone is the rock of offense.

- How do Christ's miracles allude to the call to self-denial? Why is self-denial important?

  Christ's miracles allude to self-denial because they show that even though He has come to restore and make whole (Mark 2:17), self-denial is so important that it is worth giving up the very same things that Jesus has come to restore. Even though a physical restoration of sight is wonderful, it is far more important to give up physical sight for spiritual sight. Jesus is emphatic on this point because those who do not suffer themselves in this life will endure eternal suffering in the lake of fire.

- What was the prevailing Jewish teaching on divorce in Jesus' time, and how did He respond?

  The Jewish teaching on divorce in the first century was very liberal in theory: it allowed for a man to divorce his wife simply because he was unhappy. This practice originated from the permitting of divorce in Deuteronomy 24:1–4, and the practice was made common by isolating that section of Scripture from the rest of Moses' teaching. Jesus noticed that the Jews were ignoring Scripture's broader teaching on marriage, so He responded by quoting Genesis' design for marriage as oneness before God (Gen. 1:27; 2:24), therefore proving that divorce should be the exception and not the norm.

REVIEW QUIZ

1. **A.**
   As Dr. Godfrey explained in the lecture, Jesus calls the disciples to encourage the strangers. "Do not stop [them]. . . . For the one who is not against us is for us. For truly, I say to you, whoever gives you a cup of water to drink because you belong to Christ will by no means lose his reward" (Mark 9:39–41).

2. **D.**
   Dr. Godfrey suggested that the "little ones" in Mark 9:42 are both children and strangers. This is because Mark is getting at the general idea of offense, and therefore Christians ought not to offend others, either strangers or children, by causing sin or casting burdens on them.

3. **D.**
   Jesus has the most explicit teaching about hell of these four. He has some of the most detailed descriptions about hell in the Gospels (see, for example, Matt. 5:29–30; Mark 9:43–49; Luke 16:19–31).

4. **B.**
   Jesus likely told the disciples to have salt in themselves because salt is tasty and therefore was seen as making something acceptable or pleasing by analogy (in this case, an acceptable sacrifice). Paul speaks similarly when he commands, "Let your speech always be gracious, seasoned with salt" (Col. 4:6).

5. **C.**
   Dr. Godfrey suggested that the Pharisees questioned Jesus on divorce because they probably expected a very strict answer from Him, which would take away from His popularity. They were not seeking to learn from Jesus; instead, they sought to entrap Him.

6. **B.**
   Divorce is permissible under certain conditions (see Matt. 5:31–32; 19:9). Although it is not God's design for marriage, He did give divorce to Israel on account of human sinfulness (Deut. 24:1–4).

17

The Call to Servanthood

INTRODUCTION

We long for eternal life. As Ecclesiastes 3:11 states, God has "put eternity into man's heart." But how does someone gain eternal life? A rich young man who encountered Jesus believed that he had the answer. In this lesson, Dr. Godfrey focuses on Mark 10 and Jesus' interactions with the rich young man and the nature of life in the kingdom, emphasizing the themes of salvation, servanthood, and suffering.

LEARNING GOALS

When you have finished this lesson, you should be able to:

- Explain the relationship between the rich young man and the law
- Understand what it takes to follow Christ into the kingdom
- Identify the characteristics of a true Christian leader

KEY IDEAS

- Eternal life cannot be earned by human effort—except Christ's.
- We must be willing to suffer earthly loss for the sake of the gospel.
- True greatness in God's kingdom comes from humility and service.

REFLECTION & DISCUSSION QUESTIONS

Before the Video

What Do You Think?

Take a moment to answer the following questions. They will prepare you for the lecture.

- What is the importance of the law? Is the law important for Christians today? Why or why not?

- What makes a good leader? How did Christ exemplify true leadership?

Scripture Reading

And they were exceedingly astonished, and said to him, "Then who can be saved?" Jesus looked at them and said, "With man it is impossible, but not with God. For all things are possible with God."

—Mark 10:26–27

- What language in this passage suggests that we cannot save ourselves?

During the Video

Answer the following questions while you watch the video. They will guide you through the lecture.

The Rich Young Man *0:00–12:01*

- Does Jesus deny His divinity by saying, "No one is good except God alone" (Mark 10:18)? Why or why not?

- Why does Jesus tell the man to sell everything? What is a common error in interpreting this verse?

- What is the answer to the question, "What must I do to inherit eternal life?" (Mark 10:17)?

Living for the Kingdom *12:01–25:03*

- What rewards will followers of Christ receive in this life? Are these rewards perfect?

- What did the sons of Zebedee desire, and how did Jesus respond?

After the Video

Answer the following questions after you have finished the lecture. They will help you identify and summarize the major points.

- Why does Jesus respond critically to the young man's question about eternal life? What was His purpose in doing so?

  If you are in a group, have the members discuss how Christians ought to give and receive criticism. Ask: How does this inform the way that we approach Scripture?

- Is it difficult for the rich to inherit the kingdom of God? What about the poor? Why?

  If you are in a group, have the members share a time when the kingdom of God cost them something. Ask: How did that help your growth in grace?

- According to Jesus, what should characterize the greatest disciples? How does this compare to gentile rulers? How does it apply to Jesus?

  If you are in a group, have the members discuss what actions display humble service in everyday life. Ask: How did Jesus display servanthood?

PRAYER

Commit what you have learned from God's Word in this lesson to prayer.

- Praise God for His omnipotence that works all things for good.
- Confess the times when you have sought good without God.
- Thank God for the rich mercy He has given you through Christ.
- Ask God to create a spirit of servanthood within you for the sake of others.

REVIEW QUIZ

Use these multiple-choice questions to measure what you learned from this lesson.

1. What grouping of commandments does Jesus judge the young man with?
   a. The first table of the law
   b. The second table of the law
   c. The new law
   d. Both a and b
2. Why did the rich young man go away from Jesus?
   a. He was self-centered.
   b. He wanted to check the Scriptures first.
   c. He was not truly interested in Jesus.
   d. Both a and c.
3. The disciples were surprised to learn that it is hard for a rich man to enter the kingdom.
   a. True
   b. False
4. What is likely the reason that Peter followed Christ?
   a. To earn eternal life
   b. To witness miracles
   c. Because he trusted and loved Jesus
   d. Because he knew that Jesus was the Christ
5. What verbal theme from Mark's gospel is repeated in Jesus' third prophecy?
   a. Spitting
   b. Flogging
   c. Mocking
   d. Killing
6. What historical example was given of misusing Christian leadership?
   a. Bishops in the early church
   b. The pope
   c. Martin Luther's Reformation
   d. English Nonconformity

Answer Key—The Call to Servanthood

REFLECTION & DISCUSSION QUESTIONS

Before the Video

What Do You Think?

These are personal questions. The answers should be based on your own knowledge and experience.

Scripture Reading

- What language in this passage suggests that we cannot save ourselves?

  We cannot merit salvation by our own works, and this is implied by the disciples' question, "Then who can be saved?" The expected answer is "no one," but Jesus answers with an important qualification, that although salvation is impossible for us to attain on our own, "all things are possible with God."

During the Video

The Rich Young Man

- Does Jesus deny His divinity by saying, "No one is good except God alone" (Mark 10:18)? Why or why not?

  Jesus does not deny His divinity by saying, "No one is good except God alone." The statement has a strong rhetorical purpose, and Jesus is interested in seeing whether the rich young man understands what he seeks and whether he recognizes his own emptiness and dependence on God for eternal life.

- Why does Jesus tell the man to sell everything? What is a common error in interpreting this verse?

  Discerning the man's heart, Jesus knows that his possessions truly have hold of him and that they are more important to him than Jesus is. A common misinterpretation is viewing this as a universal requirement to faithfully follow Jesus, but His call to sell everything teaches us to trust Christ with everything, which is precisely what it means to follow Him.

- What is the answer to the question, "What must I do to inherit eternal life?" (Mark 10:17)?

  While God gives eternal life to those who believe (John 3:16), He does not give it as a corresponding reward for faith, but rather bestows it as a gracious gift (Rom. 4:4–5). Instead, the only way to "earn" eternal life is by recognizing that earning it is impossible, that Christ is our Savior who has earned eternal life for His people precisely because we could not do so.

Living for the Kingdom

- What rewards will followers of Christ receive in this life? Are these rewards perfect?

  Followers of Christ will be richly blessed in this life for following Him, ultimately with spiritual blessings and not physical ones. While we may lose our family, we will gain the family of the church (see Mark 3:35). Although Christians have such spiritual blessings, they come alongside suffering, persecution, and challenges in this life.

- What did the sons of Zebedee desire, and how did Jesus respond?

  James and John, the sons of Zebedee, wanted glory with Christ, so they asked to sit next to Him in the kingdom. They wanted glory immediately, but Jesus once again revealed that suffering must precede glory and guaranteed that they would have suffering like His (Mark 10:39).

After the Video

- Why does Jesus respond critically to the young man's question about eternal life? What was His purpose in doing so?

  Jesus is critical of the young man's question about eternal life because he is trying too hard to inherit eternal life on his own terms. In the Greek, he twice mentions himself when he says, "What must I do, that I might inherit eternal life?" as Dr. Godfrey translated. Jesus responds accordingly by questioning the man's conception of goodness. This is also why, afterward, Jesus says: "With man it is impossible, but not with God. For all things are possible with God" (Mark 10:27). God is necessary for salvation, and the rich young man did not comprehend that doctrine.

- Is it difficult for the rich to inherit the kingdom of God? What about the poor? Why?

  It is difficult for the rich to inherit the kingdom of God, as Jesus says (Mark 10:23, 25), but He also implies that it is likewise difficult for the poor (v. 24). This is because the kingdom of God is difficult to enter regardless of status or wealth. Dr. Godfrey noted that Jesus "is in effect saying how difficult it is for everybody to enter the kingdom of God." Christ speaks this way to highlight the fact that, humanly speaking, salvation is impossible, but that it can be attained by the grace and power of God (v. 27).

- According to Jesus, what should characterize the greatest disciples? How does this compare to gentile rulers? How does it apply to Jesus?

  Since the disciples were quarreling over greatness again, Jesus reveals that the greatest of them ought to be known by lowliness and service to those under their authority. This contrasts with the conception of rule among the gentiles, through which authority is lorded over those in the ruler's service. There is no humble spirit of service. Here, Jesus stands to be an exemplar of such service, since that is the whole purpose of His mission (Mark 10:44). Christ came to serve, even to the point of death, whether that be in the washing of feet (John 13:1–20) or in the redemption of His people (3:13–15).

REVIEW QUIZ

1. **B.**
   Jesus quotes the second table of the Ten Commandments, which is commandments five through ten. He does this so that he can convict the young man on the human level before pointing toward God.

2. **D.**
   The rich young man departed from Jesus not because he took Christ's words seriously but because he was offended by the cost of discipleship. The man was unable to deny himself (Mark 8:34), which has been the focus of much of Jesus' teaching in Mark 9–10, and therefore he could never meaningfully follow Christ.

3. **A.**
   Although Jesus had consistently pressed the message of self-denial on the disciples, they did not understand how it applied to the rich young man. Because of this, they were surprised that Jesus said it would be difficult for the rich to enter the kingdom of God (Mark 10:23–25).

4. **C.**
   Peter seems to have followed Jesus out of simple faith and love, and not for an elaborate end or because he possessed full knowledge of Christ. Dr. Godfrey suggested this reading of the text in saying: "I think Jesus implies: 'You didn't follow Me to earn something. You followed Me because you loved Me and trusted Me.'"

5. **A.**
   Mark's gospel repeats the theme of "spitting" in Jesus' third prophecy. This contrasts with the earlier use of spit for healing (Mark 8:23–25), since now spit is used by the gentiles to ridicule and reject Christ (10:34).

6. **B.**
   Historically, the claim to the papacy has been seriously problematic for the call to servant leadership. Although the pope may claim to serve the servants of God, his public appearances and the constant glorification of his office by others are contrary to Christ's commands concerning servant leadership.

18

The King Arrives

INTRODUCTION

Jesus' triumphal entry is a pivotal moment in the Gospels. Jesus is heralded as King as He enters Jerusalem, yet Jesus does not arrive at Jerusalem only as King but as Israel's true Prophet and Priest. In this lesson, Dr. Godfrey looks at the healing of Bartimaeus and at Jesus' initial ministry in Jerusalem that focuses on Israel's unfaithfulness and futile hopes in the temple.

LEARNING GOALS

When you have finished this lesson, you should be able to:

- Explain the significance of Bartimaeus' interaction with Jesus as contrasted with Jesus' encounter with the rich young man
- Understand the symbolic importance of Jesus' actions in Jerusalem
- Identify key allusions to Old Testament prophecies fulfilled through Jesus' ministry

KEY IDEAS

- Genuine faith perseveres despite societal opposition.
- Jesus is Israel's true Prophet, Priest, and King.
- The Old Testament temple and sacrificial system find their ultimate fulfillment in Christ.

REFLECTION & DISCUSSION QUESTIONS

Before the Video

What Do You Think?

Take a moment to answer the following questions. They will prepare you for the lecture.

- Why did Jesus heal the blind? How can their stories inspire faith in us?

- Why is Jerusalem important in the Bible? How does it relate to Jesus?

Scripture Reading

"Go into the village in front of you, and immediately as you enter it you will find a colt tied, on which no one has ever sat. Untie it and bring it. If anyone says to you, 'Why are you doing this?' say, 'The Lord has need of it and will send it back here immediately.'" And they went away and found a colt tied at a door outside in the street, and they untied it. And some of those standing there said to them, "What are you doing, untying the colt?" And they told them what Jesus had said, and they let them go.

—Mark 11:2–6

- How is Jesus' kingship already on display in His preparations to enter Jerusalem?

During the Video

Answer the following questions while you watch the video. They will guide you through the lecture.

Bartimaeus *0:00–12:08*

- Why is it significant that Mark records Bartimaeus' name? Compare this to other people who interacted with Jesus.

- What is the importance of Bartimaeus' cloak? Why would a cloak be notable in the ancient world?

Israel's True Prophet, Priest, and King *12:08–24:34*

- What is the chiastic center of Mark 11–13? What theme does it portray?

- What is the significance of Jesus' entering Jerusalem on a colt? What does this reveal about Him?

After the Video

Answer the following questions after you have finished the lecture. They will help you identify and summarize the major points.

- Why is Bartimaeus' faith noteworthy? How does it exemplify the call to faith?

  If you are in a group, have the members discuss the relationship between faith and sight. Ask: How does this apply to Bartimaeus?

- What is Jesus' relationship to prophecy? How can Jesus' role as Prophet encourage us?

  If you are in a group, have some of the members share a prophecy from the Bible that has encouraged them. Ask: How does it connect to Christ?

- Why does Jesus curse the fig tree? What do figs symbolize in the Old Testament?

  If you are in a group, have the members discuss the importance of bearing fruit in the Christian life. Ask: Why should we bear fruit, since Jesus has already redeemed us?

PRAYER

Commit what you have learned from God's Word in this lesson to prayer.

- Praise God for His sovereign rule over creation and for the authority that was given to Jesus Christ.
- Confess anything that you cling to that keeps you from a deeper devotion to Christ.
- Thank God for giving you the perfect Prophet, Priest, and King in Christ.
- Ask God to help you, by His Spirit, let go of anything that hinders your devotion so that you might bear true spiritual fruit.

REVIEW QUIZ

Use these multiple-choice questions to measure what you learned from this lesson.

1. What unique title does Bartimaeus call Jesus by?
   a. Son of God
   b. Son of David
   c. Son of Man
   d. Son of Joseph
2. Why does Mark say that "it was already late" when Jesus entered Jerusalem (Mark 11:11)?
   a. Because, simply, the day was late
   b. Because it was late in human history
   c. Because it was late for Jerusalem and the temple
   d. Both a and c
3. The stones of the Second Temple are still standing today.
   a. True
   b. False
4. Which office or offices of Christ did Dr. Godfrey most emphasize in this lesson?
   a. Prophet
   b. Priest
   c. King
   d. Both a and c
5. What action does the theme of "futility" best describe?
   a. The Jews' clinging to the temple
   b. The Roman crucifixion of Jesus
   c. Judas' betrayal of Jesus
   d. Jewish ritual washings
6. Which psalm prophesies of Jesus in Jerusalem?
   a. Psalm 117
   b. Psalm 118
   c. Psalm 119
   d. Psalm 121

Answer Key—The King Arrives

REFLECTION & DISCUSSION QUESTIONS

Before the Video

What Do You Think?

These are personal questions. The answers should be based on your own knowledge and experience.

Scripture Reading

- How is Jesus' kingship already on display in His preparations to enter Jerusalem?

  We see Jesus' authority as King on display in this passage in many ways. The disciples are obedient to His request, but the people who owned the colt also seemingly hand it over for the Lord's use without question.

During the Video

Bartimaeus

- Why is it significant that Mark records Bartimaeus' name? Compare this to other people who interacted with Jesus.

  It is significant that Bartimaeus' name is mentioned because he is not of a high calling or status. Mark's recording of names is important, so the lack of a name for either the rich young man or the previous blind man is significant when compared to Bartimaeus. It may well be that Bartimaeus later had a position in the church and that people knew about him. Ultimately, Jesus knows him and knows him by name.

- What is the importance of Bartimaeus' cloak? Why would a cloak be notable in the ancient world?

  Bartimaeus' cloak is important because cloaks were very difficult to make in the ancient world. This was also significant because Bartimaeus, being poor, would not have owned much else. By throwing off his cloak, he shows how much his faith was truly worth.

Israel's True Prophet, Priest, and King

- What is the chiastic center of Mark 11–13? What theme does it portray?

  The Jerusalem chiasm (Mark 11–13) centers on the parable of the tenants. Jesus is highlighting Israel's unfaithfulness and the sinfulness of its leaders. This points toward the theme of futility and Israel's rebellious history. The people of Israel, like unruly tenants, rejected God's authority over them and rejected the prophets that He had sent them.

- What is the significance of Jesus' entering Jerusalem on a colt? What does this reveal about Him?

  Jesus enters Jerusalem on a colt to fulfill the prophecy of Zechariah 9:9. This action proclaims His identity as both King and Prophet. Amazingly, Jesus, as Prophet, foretold exactly where His disciples would find the colt.

After the Video

- Why is Bartimaeus' faith noteworthy? How does it exemplify the call to faith?

  Bartimaeus' faith is commendable because of its persistence and depth. First, he was told not to come to Jesus by others, but he cried out and came to Christ anyway (Mark 10:48–50). Furthermore, people such as the rich young man could not give everything away when asked to do so, but Bartimaeus gave away all that he had without anybody's urging him, "throwing off his cloak" (v. 50). Finally, despite being blind, he could clearly see who Jesus was, showing that he walked by faith and not by sight (see 2 Cor. 5:7).

- What is Jesus' relationship to prophecy? How can Jesus' role as Prophet encourage us?

  Mark wants us to see that not only is Jesus the fulfiller of prophecy, but He is the Prophet. This truth has a rich application. Because Jesus is both Prophet and fulfillment, we can trust Him, for He always accomplishes what He promises and sets out to do.

- Why does Jesus curse the fig tree? What do figs symbolize in the Old Testament?

  In the Old Testament, Israel is compared to a fig tree. Jesus curses the fig tree because it does not have any fruit, and it was symbolic of Israel. When Jesus is checking to see whether the fig tree has fruit, He is picturing for us what is happening in His earthly ministry and time in Jerusalem.

REVIEW QUIZ

1. **B.**
   Bartimaeus calls Jesus the "Son of David" (Mark 10:47–48) because Jesus is the King who fulfills the Davidic covenant. This is significant because it is the first time that someone calls Jesus by this title in Mark's gospel, in anticipation of the triumphal entry.

2. **D.**
   Mark says that it was already late when Jesus entered Jerusalem, not only because the day was coming to a close, but also because it was spiritually late for Jerusalem. The time was fulfilled and judgment was imminent.

3. **B.**
   Although the Wailing Wall of Jerusalem is still standing, this wall was only part of the Temple Mount and not the temple itself. On the contrary, the entirety of the temple was destroyed in AD 70, just as Jesus prophesied in Mark 13:2.

4. **D.**
   While Dr. Godfrey did tie Israel's futile hope in the temple to Jesus' arrival as the true Priest and final sacrifice, he most strongly emphasized the kingly and prophetic offices of Christ in this lesson. Jesus was heralded as King in the encounter with Bartimaeus and during the triumphal entry, and He was shown to be Prophet in His prophecy about the colt and in speaking out against Jerusalem.

5. **A.**
   Dr. Godfrey described the way that the Jews clung to the temple as especially futile. They did not understand that the goal of the temple and the law was its fulfillment in Christ (Rom. 10:4), and consequently they persisted in futility instead of faith.

6. **B.**
   Psalm 118 directly applies to Jesus' ministry in Jerusalem in multiple ways. First, it is the psalm that is sung about Him in the triumphal entry (Mark 11:9–10). Second, Jesus quotes verses 22 and 23 at the end of the parable of the tenants. This shows that the message of this psalm is central to Jesus' mission and work in Jerusalem.

19

Israel's Rejection

INTRODUCTION

Throughout the Old Testament, Israel vacillated between obedience to and rebellion against God. But how would the people respond now that God had sent His only Son to them? In this lesson, Dr. Godfrey continues to focus on Jesus' ministry in Jerusalem before His crucifixion, especially on Jesus' pronouncement of judgment on Israel.

LEARNING GOALS

When you have finished this lesson, you should be able to:

- Understand the purpose of the temple
- Explain the relationship between faith and prayer
- Identify examples of the theme of futility in this section of Mark's gospel

KEY IDEAS

- Jesus demonstrates His authority over worship and the temple by cleansing it.
- True faith has God and His purposes as its object.
- Jesus answers the Pharisees according to their folly, lest they be wise in their own eyes.

REFLECTION & DISCUSSION QUESTIONS

Before the Video

What Do You Think?

Take a moment to answer the following questions. They will prepare you for the lecture.

- What was the purpose of the temple in Israel? What is the purpose of the church for God's people today?
- Why is faith necessary for prayer?

Scripture Reading

"Therefore I tell you, whatever you ask in prayer, believe that you have received it, and it will be yours. And whenever you stand praying, forgive, if you have anything against anyone, so that your Father also who is in heaven may forgive you your trespasses."

—Mark 11:24–25

- What does Jesus command for efficacious prayer?

During the Video

Answer the following questions while you watch the video. They will guide you through the lecture.

Faith and Figs *0:00–14:52*

- Was it lawful for Jesus to cleanse the temple? Why or why not?
- Why did the chief priests not stop Jesus from cleansing the temple?
- Will Christ give you anything you desire if you ask with unwavering faith? Why or why not?

Against the Pharisees *14:52–24:58*

- Why did Jesus' question about John the Baptist trap the Pharisees? Why was it effective?
- What is another nuance of the Greek word for "appearances" (Mark 12:14)? Why might this be significant?

After the Video

Answer the following questions after you have finished the lecture. They will help you identify and summarize the major points.

- What virtue does the fig tree point toward? What does this mean for Christians?

  If you are in a group, have the members give an example of an important symbol in Scripture and describe what it means.
- What mountain is Jesus alluding to when speaking about faith? Why is that important for the promise of casting it into the sea?

  If you are in a group, ask the members about a time when they witnessed the power of faith. Ask: How should we orient our faith when praying for ourselves or others?
- Explain how Psalm 118 prophesies about Jesus. What events and roles of Christ does it reveal?

  If you are in a group, ask the members why the Psalms are important to Jesus' ministry. Ask: What value can Christians glean from the Psalms today?

PRAYER

Commit what you have learned from God's Word in this lesson to prayer.

- Praise God for His dwelling with us through His Son.
- Confess ways that you have misvalued the church.
- Thank God for the gift of faith and the Spirit's work in your life.
- Ask God to characterize your church's worship with spirit and truth.

REVIEW QUIZ

Use these multiple-choice questions to measure what you learned from this lesson.

1. What did Jesus intend to show by cleansing the temple?
   a. That it is a place for sacrificial offerings
   b. That it is a home for all nations
   c. That it is the most sacred place on earth
   d. That it is a house of prayer
2. What psalm might Jesus be alluding to when He says that faith can move mountains?
   a. Psalm 31
   b. Psalm 32
   c. Psalm 46
   d. Psalm 51
3. Forgiveness is a necessary aspect of prayer.
   a. True
   b. False
4. What did the Pharisees care most about?
   a. The truth
   b. The people
   c. Their position
   d. Their rituals
5. Whom does the son represent in the parable of the tenants?
   a. John the Baptist
   b. Jesus
   c. The church
   d. The Pharisees
6. What kind of questions were the Pharisees and Herodians asking Jesus?
   a. Scriptural questions
   b. Inquisitive questions
   c. Difficult questions
   d. Dishonest questions

Answer Key—Israel's Rejection

REFLECTION & DISCUSSION QUESTIONS

Before the Video

What Do You Think?

These are personal questions. The answers should be based on your own knowledge and experience.

Scripture Reading

- *What does Jesus command for efficacious prayer?*

  In this passage, Jesus commands two things for efficacious prayer. First, He calls all who pray to faith, as Hebrews declares, "Without faith it is impossible to please [God]" (11:6). Second, He commands those who entreat God in prayer to also forgive others because God has forgiven them.

During the Video

Faith and Figs

- Was it lawful for Jesus to cleanse the temple? Why or why not?

  It was lawful for Jesus to cleanse the temple because of His authority over it. He, as the Prophet, had the right to declare what the real point of the temple was and to drive out those who were violating it. He is the One who delivers the Word of God to the house of God.

- Why did the chief priests not stop Jesus from cleansing the temple?

  The chief priests did not stop Jesus from cleansing the temple because they were afraid of the crowd. They did not dare to challenge Him. Though they rejected Him and had power to apprehend Him, they could not do so without inciting the crowd.

- Will Christ give you anything you desire if you ask with unwavering faith? Why or why not?

  Even though Jesus gives the example of a mountain being thrown into the sea because of true faith (Mark 11:23), it is important to keep in mind that before this statement is the command to "have faith in God" (v. 22). Faith in God will always desire His will and not our own (Matt. 6:10), which is why faith won't give us just any worldly desire that we might have, but instead, faith gives Christians whatever God's will is for His glory and our good.

Against the Pharisees

- Why did Jesus' question about John the Baptist trap the Pharisees? Why was it effective?

  Jesus' question about John the Baptist was effective against the Pharisees because the same leaders who hated Jesus also hated John, so they could not answer that John's baptism was from above. After all, they had rejected him. They also could not answer that his baptism was from man because they feared angering the crowd.

- What is another nuance of the Greek word for "appearances" (Mark 12:14)? Why might this be significant?

  Another nuance of the Greek word for "appearances" is the word "face," with the intent of showing that Jesus is not swayed by someone's looks. This is also significant because Jesus is about to mention faces in relation to taxes (Mark 12:16), which shows that Mark is subtly introducing some wordplay into the passage dealing with outward appearances and true loyalty.

After the Video

- What virtue does the fig tree point toward? What does this mean for Christians?

  The fig tree represents the power of faith. Jesus uses this anecdote to teach that true faith is powerful and can accomplish its purpose. When you trust the Lord and are oriented to His purpose and your desire is to serve Him, then when you pray to be able to serve Him, He will enable you to serve Him. Efficacious prayer is that the work of the Lord might be done.

- What mountain is Jesus alluding to when speaking about faith? Why is that important for the promise of casting it into the sea?

  When Jesus speaks of casting a mountain into the sea (Mark 11:23), he is talking about Mount Zion. This is significant because it is the same Temple Mount that Jesus was on. Dr. Godfrey noted that the minute He left the temple, the sellers would bring all their wares back. This sad reality is part of the reason that Jesus singles out Mount Zion, because it is ultimately a call to see whether one's will is aligned with God's. God's will was to destroy the temple because of idolatry.

- Explain how Psalm 118 prophesies about Jesus. What events and roles of Christ does it reveal?

  Psalm 118 prophesies concerning Jesus in multiple ways. First, part of it was sung for Jesus' triumphal entry (v. 26). Second, it prophesies the death and resurrection of Christ when it says, "The stone that the builders rejected has become the cornerstone" (v. 22), which has historically been understood to refer to Christ's resurrection after the crucifixion. This ultimately means that now He is the cornerstone and head of the whole church (Eph. 2:20), which Dr. Godfrey described as the "essential element of salvation."

REVIEW QUIZ

1. **D.**
   By cleansing the temple and quoting from the prophet Isaiah, Jesus asserted His authority as Israel's true Prophet and declared that the temple's purpose was worship and prayer and not commerce.

2. **C.**
   Jesus may be alluding to Psalm 46 when He tells the disciples that faith can move "this mountain" into the sea (Mark 11:23). Psalm 46 similarly states, "Therefore we will not fear though the earth gives way, though the mountains be moved into the heart of the sea" (Ps. 46:2).

3. **A.**
   Forgiveness is a necessary component of prayer; Jesus commands the disciples to forgive others when they pray (Matt. 6:12–15; 11:25).

4. **C.**
   The Pharisees were concerned about their own position and power more than anything else. If they had cared about the truth or the people, they would have told Jesus that John's baptism was from man, but instead, they sought only to defend themselves and their power, so they claimed ignorance (Mark 11:32–33).

5. **B.**
   The son in the parable of the tenants represents Jesus. This is why the parable calls Him "a beloved son" (Mark 12:6), which harks back to the Father's words during Jesus' baptism and transfiguration.

6. **D.**
   The Pharisees and Herodians were asking Jesus dishonest questions as they sought "to trap him in his talk" (Mark 12:13).

20

Jesus Questioned

INTRODUCTION

In Jerusalem, Jesus is confronted by Pharisees, Sadducees, and scribes who pose questions to entrap Him and turn people against Him. How will Jesus answer? In this lesson, Dr. Godfrey takes us through Jesus' responses and how they reveal His wisdom, authority, and understanding of God's Word.

LEARNING GOALS

When you have finished this lesson, you should be able to:

- Recognize Jesus' profound wisdom in answering His opponents
- Identify the motives behind the different groups questioning Jesus
- Explain the difference between true and hypocritical worship

KEY IDEAS

- Jesus' teaching on rendering to Caesar what belongs to Caesar underscores how Christians are to honor both God and civil authorities.
- The doctrine of the resurrection is firmly rooted in the Old Testament, as demonstrated by Jesus' response to the Sadducees.
- The heart of the law is love of God and love of neighbor.

REFLECTION & DISCUSSION QUESTIONS

Before the Video

What Do You Think?

Take a moment to answer the following questions. They will prepare you for the lecture.

- Why will God resurrect our bodies?

- How should Christians navigate our relationship to civil authorities?

Scripture Reading

And one of the scribes came up and heard them disputing with one another, and seeing that he answered them well, asked him, "Which commandment is the most important of all?" Jesus answered, "The most important is, 'Hear, O Israel: The Lord our God, the Lord is one. And you shall love the Lord your God with all your heart and with all your soul and with all your mind and with all your strength.'"

—Mark 12:28–30

- What do even the scribes recognize about Jesus? What might His answer to their question reveal about Him?

During the Video

Answer the following questions while you watch the video. They will guide you through the lecture.

Authority and Revelation *0:00–12:54*

- How does Jesus respond to the Pharisees' question about taxes? What Old Testament text does this bring to mind?

- What is fundamentally flawed in the Sadducees' question about marriage?

Scribes and the Law *12:54–24:41*

- How does Jesus' answer to the scribe reveal the heart of the Mosaic law?

- How does Jesus challenge the scribes? Why does He do so?

After the Video

Answer the following questions after you have finished the lecture. They will help you identify and summarize the major points.

- Why did the Sadducees object to the resurrection?

  If you are in a group, have the members discuss why the resurrection is important to Christianity. Ask: How can the hope of resurrection affect our day-to-day lives?

- How does Jesus prove the resurrection from Exodus?

  If you are in a group, have the members explain an important connection between the Old and New Testaments. Ask: Why is it important to keep the two united?

- How was the scribe sympathetic to Jesus, and how was he only close to the kingdom?

  If you are in a group, have the members give an example of someone who is both near and far from the gospel. Ask: How does this expand our understanding of people and the gospel?

PRAYER

Commit what you have learned from God's Word in this lesson to prayer.

- Praise God for His incomprehensible wisdom and unsearchable knowledge.
- Confess the ways that you doubt and question Jesus instead of seeking and loving Him.
- Thank God for sending His Spirit to inspire the Scriptures and lead you into all truth.
- Ask God to give you a love for His Word and a passion for Jesus.

REVIEW QUIZ

Use these multiple-choice questions to measure what you learned from this lesson.

1. Jesus divides the world into the sacred and the secular.
   a. True
   b. False
2. Which books of the Old Testament did the Sadducees accept?
   a. The Law
   b. The Prophets
   c. The Writings
   d. All of the above
3. In the resurrection, what is one way that humans will be like angels?
   a. Humans will become angels.
   b. Humans will be immaterial.
   c. Humans will be taught by angels.
   d. Humans will not procreate.
4. What was the fundamental goal of the Mosaic religion?
   a. Sacrifices and the temple
   b. Love for the nations
   c. Love for God
   d. Sacrifices in love
5. In which psalm does David prophesy about Jesus?
   a. Psalm 32
   b. Psalm 51
   c. Psalm 89
   d. Psalm 110
6. How did the crowds react to Jesus' dispute with the scribes?
   a. They heard Him gladly and with much commotion.
   b. They heard Him gladly and silently.
   c. They heard Him angrily and with much commotion.
   d. They heard Him angrily and silently.

Answer Key—Jesus Questioned

REFLECTION & DISCUSSION QUESTIONS

Before the Video

What Do You Think?

These are personal questions. The answers should be based on your own knowledge and experience.

Scripture Reading

- What do even the scribes recognize about Jesus? What might His answer to their question reveal about Him?

  Many attempted to trap Jesus with their questions, but here the scribes acknowledge that He "answered them well" (Mark 12:28). This may have led to a genuine question about the heart of the law, even if to test Jesus. What we see from Jesus' answers, here and elsewhere, is that His use of Scripture cannot be refuted. His answer displays His mastery of God's Word and His absolute commitment to the truth.

During the Video

Authority and Revelation

- How does Jesus respond to the Pharisees' question about taxes? What Old Testament text does this bring to mind?

  Jesus responds to the Pharisees' question by asking why they test Him (Mark 12:15). Jesus does this because He knows that the question is not genuine but hypocritical. His response alludes to the rebellion at Meribah in Exodus 17, where the Israelites likewise tested God and became a negative example for all their descendants (Ps. 95:7–9).

- What is fundamentally flawed in the Sadducees' question about marriage?

  Jesus makes clear in His teaching against the Sadducees that they do not understand the nature of creation or the nature of marriage. Jesus fully affirms the resurrection against their beliefs, but He defends it by showing how there is a disconnect between life in this world and life in the world to come. The issues that the Sadducees have with marriage are based in their false views about the resurrection and misunderstanding that life after the resurrection will be the same as it is now.

Scribes and the Law

- How does Jesus' answer to the scribe reveal the heart of the Mosaic law?

  Jesus' answer to the scribe reveals the heart of the Mosaic law by emphasizing that love is the essence and fulfillment of the law. When asked by the scribe which commandment is the most important, Jesus responds by quoting the Shema from Deuteronomy 6:4–5 and Leviticus 19:18. Often when we think of the Mosaic law, we think of its elaborate ceremonies and sacrifices, but at its heart is the simplicity of love.

- How does Jesus challenge the scribes? Why does He do so?

  Jesus challenges the scribes both theologically and practically. Theologically, He addresses their expectations of the Messiah, and practically, He confronts their limited interpretations of the law. The scribes want a political Messiah, but Jesus shows that the Messiah has a greater authority. The scribes are notorious hypocrites, so Jesus denounces their outward displays of piety that mask their lawlessness.

After the Video

- Why did the Sadducees object to the resurrection?

  The Sadducees objected to the resurrection out of their strict adherence to the Torah, the first five books of the Bible, which they believed did not teach the resurrection. They also deemed it to be absurd, and so they presented a hypothetical situation to draw out this absurdity: if marriage can occur multiple times in this life, they objected, to whom would a woman be married in the resurrection?

- How does Jesus prove the resurrection from Exodus?

  Jesus proves the resurrection from Exodus by quoting God's saying, "I am the God of your father, the God of Abraham, the God of Isaac, and the God of Jacob" (3:6). Jesus uses the verb "I am" to show that God is the God of Abraham, Isaac, and Jacob in the present and not in the past. This is profound because it challenges the Sadducees' assumption that life is temporary and that the soul dies with the body. Furthermore, Jesus strikes at the heart of the Sadducees' beliefs by quoting from the Torah, instead of quoting from other Old Testament texts on the resurrection, such as Daniel 12:2.

- How was the scribe sympathetic to Jesus, and how was he only close to the kingdom?

  The scribe seems to have genuinely sought answers from Jesus, "seeing that he answered them well" (Mark 12:28), yet he still retained a skeptical attitude, which is why Matthew notes that he asked the question "to test him" (Matt. 22:35). While the scribe was close to the kingdom because he understood the essential aspect of the law and Mark mentions that Jesus considered his answer wise, the scribe did not further inquire how to enter into the kingdom.

REVIEW QUIZ

1. **B.**
   Although Jesus makes a distinction between what belongs to God and what belongs to Caesar, He is ultimately saying that everything belongs to God, such that the coin with the idolatrous image of Caesar ought to be returned to Caesar out of reverence for God.

2. **A.**
   The Sadducees accepted only the Torah or Law, which is the first five books of the Old Testament. This is important because it is part of the reason why they rejected the resurrection, believing that the Torah did not teach it.

3. **D.**
   In the resurrection, humans will be like angels in that they will not procreate. God created angels, yet He did not create them to procreate with each other. This is a function of marriage, but in the resurrection, as Jesus teaches, we "neither marry nor are given in marriage, but are like angels in heaven" (Mark 12:25).

4. **C.**
   While all of these are found in various parts of the law of Moses, the fundamental goal of the Mosaic law was love for God, and after that, love for neighbor. This is why Jesus remarks that they are the most important commands (Mark 12:29–31), and the scribe also agrees that they are greater than sacrifices (vv. 32–33).

5. **D.**
   David prophesies about Jesus in Psalm 110 when he writes, "The Lord says to my Lord: 'Sit at my right hand, until I make your enemies your footstool'" (Ps. 110:1). This shows Jesus' greater authority, that despite being born from the line of David according to His humanity, He is the divine Messiah and not the merely political one that the scribes desire.

6. **B.**
   The crowds reacted to Jesus' conversation with the scribes with silence and gladness. "No one dared to ask him any more questions" (Mark 12:34), because they could not debate with Jesus and His command of the Scriptures. Yet they also heard Him gladly, even if Mark does not explain why (v. 37).

21

The Call to Faithfulness

INTRODUCTION

Throughout history, Christians have grappled with understanding prophecy and its relationship to future events. In this lesson, Dr. Godfrey demonstrates how the focus of Jesus' teachings in Mark 13 is not primarily about the distant end of the world but about a near event—the destruction of the temple—and the call for faithfulness amid trials.

LEARNING GOALS

When you have finished this lesson, you should be able to:

- Understand the primary fulfillment of Jesus' prophecy in Mark 13
- Identify how Jesus calls His followers to faithfulness
- Explain the relationship between the disciples' experience and the great tribulation

KEY IDEAS

- The temple and its impending destruction are central to Jesus' prophecy in Mark.
- True faith will always persevere to the end.
- Jesus is working now to gather His elect from every corner of the earth.

REFLECTION & DISCUSSION QUESTIONS

Before the Video

What Do You Think?

Take a moment to answer the following questions. They will prepare you for the lecture.

- What would you value more and why: knowing the details of what is going to happen in the future or faithfulness in any circumstance?

- How has misunderstanding of biblical prophecy led to confusion or false teaching?

Scripture Reading

"Truly, I say to you, this generation will not pass away until all these things take place. Heaven and earth will pass away, but my words will not pass away."

—Mark 13:30–31

- How does Jesus describe the quality of His words?

During the Video

Answer the following questions while you watch the video. They will guide you through the lecture.

Faith amid Trials *0:00–13:12*

- Is Mark 13 primarily about "Signs of the End of the Age"? Why or why not?

- What danger did Jesus warn His disciples about?

The Great Tribulation *13:12–24:03*

- What is the "great tribulation"? Considering this, what must we be careful of in our interpretation of Scripture?

- What key phrase helps us situate the time frame of Jesus' prophecy in Mark 13?

After the Video

Answer the following questions after you have finished the lecture. They will help you identify and summarize the major points.

- How does Matthew's version of the Olivet Discourse compare with Mark's use of and intention for it?

  If you are in a group, have the members discuss why the Gospel writers might present Jesus' life and teaching differently. Ask: How does having multiple Gospels help us have a better understanding of Scripture and Jesus' life?

- What is Jesus' reason for telling His disciples what is soon to come? What will be the result if they heed His warning?

  If you are in a group, have the members give an example of Christian perseverance that has inspired them. Ask: How can that example help *you* persevere?

- In what way do the disciples witness the coming of the Son of Man? How does this apply to Christian history?

  If you are in a group, ask the members why it is important to stay humble about the second coming. Ask: How can it be helpful to *not* know certain things?

PRAYER

Commit what you have learned from God's Word in this lesson to prayer.

- Praise God for His sovereign control over the future.
- Confess the areas in your life in which you are not remaining watchful.
- Thank God for His Son and Spirit, that we might endure faithfully to the end.
- Ask God to give you a spirit of wakefulness so that the temptations and trials in this life do not take you by surprise.

REVIEW QUIZ

Use these multiple-choice questions to measure what you learned from this lesson.

1. Why did Dr. Godfrey criticize the heading "Signs of the End of the Age," which is often found in Bibles in Mark 13?
    a. Because it contradicts the gospel of Matthew
    b. Because it ignores Jesus' role as not only Prophet but King
    c. Because it is not specific about historical details that are in the passage
    d. Because it misleads readers into focusing on eschatology instead of faithfulness

2. Some of the events of Mark 13 are fulfilled in the book of Acts.
    a. True
    b. False

3. Which group of people fled Jerusalem when the temple was destroyed?
    a. Pharisees
    b. Sadducees
    c. Judaizers
    d. Christians

4. Which Roman general destroyed the temple in AD 70?
    a. Augustus
    b. Domitian
    c. Nero
    d. Titus

5. Why was Jesus' prophecy of the destruction of the temple so shocking?
    a. It was an architectural marvel.
    b. It had been built by Solomon, the son of David.
    c. It signified God's presence among His people.
    d. It had just been cleansed by Jesus.

6. Which Old Testament passage parallels Jesus' warning about false prophets?
    a. Numbers 12
    b. Deuteronomy 13
    c. Joel 2
    d. Zechariah 13

Answer Key—The Call to Faithfulness

REFLECTION & DISCUSSION QUESTIONS

Before the Video

What Do You Think?

These are personal questions. The answers should be based on your own knowledge and experience.

Scripture Reading

- How does Jesus describe the quality of His words?

  This passage affirms the certainty of Jesus' words, that they will never pass away. Profoundly, Jesus assures us that His words are even more established than heaven and earth.

During the Video

Faith amid Trials

- Is Mark 13 primarily about "Signs of the End of the Age"? Why or why not?

  Although many Bibles influence an interpretation of Mark 13 that focuses on the end of the age, Mark is more interested in the imminent destruction of the temple than in the end of the age. Mark's focus is the immediate context rather than a distant future eschatology.

- What danger did Jesus warn His disciples about?

  Jesus urged the disciples to remain vigilant and not be led astray because there would be much false teaching and many messianic pretenders after Him (Mark 13:5–6). This also shows why the immediate context should remain in view in Mark 13. Jesus was telling His disciples about what was approaching in the near future to protect them.

The Great Tribulation

- What is the "great tribulation"? Considering this, what must we be careful of in our interpretation of Scripture?

  Dr. Godfrey shows that the "great tribulation" is best understood as the destruction of the temple. We must be careful about giving priority to our day and age, assuming that prophecy must be fulfilled in our present moment. In this case, Jesus was talking about something that was fulfilled in our past.

- What key phrase helps us situate the time frame of Jesus' prophecy in Mark 13?

  Jesus says, "This generation will not pass away until all these things take place" (Mark 13:30). The phrase "this generation" helps us to see that He is speaking of the destruction of the temple and what the Apostles would soon experience.

After the Video

- How does Matthew's version of the Olivet Discourse compare with Mark's use of and intention for it?

  Mark 13 is primarily about the destruction of the temple and the various trials and signs associated with it. On the other hand, the Olivet Discourse as found in Matthew 24–25 contains a broader version of this discourse, which has details not only about the temple but also about the second coming of Jesus and the end of the age. This is helpful because it shows, by what Mark includes, the clear purpose of the discourse in his gospel.

- What is Jesus' reason for telling His disciples what is soon to come? What will be the result if they heed His warning?

  Jesus' reason for telling His disciples what is soon to come is that they might remain faithful, that they would be vigilant and awake, ever watchful for the trials to come. If they remain faithful, Jesus promises, the end of their endurance will be salvation (Mark 13:13). The point of this prophecy is the call to faith, and true faith will always persevere (see Heb. 3:14).

- In what way do the disciples witness the coming of the Son of Man? How does this apply to Christian history?

  Mark 13:26–27 says: "They will see the Son of Man coming in clouds with great power and glory. And then he will send out the angels and gather his elect from the four winds, from the ends of the earth to the ends of heaven." Dr. Godfrey argued that this is more about the general coming of God's kingdom than about a one-time visible event. To support this, he quoted Mark 14, where Jesus gives the high priest a similar prophecy: "You will see the Son of Man seated at the right hand of Power, and coming with the clouds of heaven" (Mark 14:62). What seems to be in view here is seeing His resurrection glory, His ascension glory, and His Pentecostal glory, as He sends power into the world that will carry the gospel out. In light of this, the Son of Man's gathering the elect signifies what happens as the course of history goes forward.

REVIEW QUIZ

1. **D.**
   The title "Signs of the End of the Age" naturally makes one think of the end of the world, which shifts our focus away from the immediacy of Jesus' prophecy in Mark 13.

2. **A.**
   Some major events of this passage are fulfilled in the book of Acts, for the Apostles are imprisoned and killed, as Jesus prophesied (see Acts 12:2–3).

3. **D.**
   Early Christians fled Jerusalem when the temple was destroyed in AD 70 in response to their knowledge of Jesus' prophecy, and consequently they understood that they were to flee when such things took place, as Jesus commanded (Mark 13:14).

4. **D.**
   The Roman general Titus was responsible for the destruction of the temple in AD 70. Titus Flavius Vespasianus would go on to become the Roman emperor, ruling from 79 to 81.

5. **C.**
   The temple symbolized God's dwelling among His people. Its destruction signified the end of an age and demonstrated the futility of Israel's hope apart from Christ.

6. **B.**
   Deuteronomy 13 best parallels what Jesus taught about false prophets and their signs, because Deuteronomy 13 admits that such prophets may even carry out marvelous signs, but if their teaching does not accord with God's Word or, as in Mark 13, Christ's teaching, then they are not from God.

22

The Night of Jesus' Betrayal

INTRODUCTION

As Jesus approached the end of His earthly ministry, He shared a final, deeply meaningful night with His disciples. This night, which includes the Last Supper, is rich with theological doctrines that have been debated for centuries. In this lesson, Dr. Godfrey looks at Jesus' last night and meal, especially focusing on His anointing, betrayal, and institution of the Lord's Supper.

LEARNING GOALS

When you have finished this lesson, you should be able to:

- Recognize the chiastic structure in Mark 14
- Distinguish between genuine and false repentance
- Explain the various positions on the Lord's Supper

KEY IDEAS

- The anointing of Jesus by the woman with costly ointment symbolizes her devotion to Christ and the preparation of His body for burial.
- Jesus is progressively forsaken, most heinously by Judas Iscariot, whose betrayal is contrasted with Peter's denial and highlights the difference between false and genuine repentance.
- Jesus instituted the Lord's Supper as the ongoing meal by which the Lord feeds and sustains His people.

REFLECTION & DISCUSSION QUESTIONS

Before the Video

What Do You Think?

Take a moment to answer the following questions. They will prepare you for the lecture.

- What makes repentance genuine? How can you tell false repentance from true repentance?
- What is the Lord's Supper? Why do Christians practice it? Does it do anything?

Scripture Reading

And as they were eating, he took bread, and after blessing it broke it and gave it to them, and said, "Take; this is my body." And he took a cup, and when he had given thanks he gave it to them, and they all drank of it. And he said to them, "This is my blood of the covenant, which is poured out for many."

—Mark 14:22–24

- What elements did Jesus use at the Last Supper? What do they represent and communicate?

During the Video

Answer the following questions while you watch the video. They will guide you through the lecture.

The Plot against Jesus *0:00–12:56*

- What did the religious leaders resolve to do during Passover? How did they intend to carry out their plan?
- Why did Judas betray Jesus? Is understanding why important for our understanding of the Last Supper?

The Last Supper *12:56–24:16*

- Where did Jesus tell His disciples to go for the Passover meal? What does this command show?

- For whom did Jesus shed His blood, and why is this important?

After the Video

Answer the following questions after you have finished the lecture. They will help you identify and summarize the major points.

- How does the woman's ointment relate to the death of Christ? Why is this important?

  If you are in a group, have the members discuss why this woman is so highly esteemed in the Gospels. Ask: How can we imitate her example?

- Compare and contrast Judas and Peter. What is the crucial difference between them?

  If you are in a group, have the members share an example of repentance and explain whether it is true or false repentance. Ask: What does true repentance always require?

- What are the four main perspectives on the Lord's Supper? Briefly explain each.

  If you are in a group, have the members reflect on how they experience the Lord's Supper. Ask: What questions do you still have about the nature of the Lord's Supper?

PRAYER

Commit what you have learned from God's Word in this lesson to prayer.

- Praise God for the union you have with Christ in the Lord's Supper.
- Confess the times when your repentance to God has not been genuine.
- Thank God for the remission of your sins through the body and blood of His only Son.
- Ask God to give you a deeper sense of communion with Him and others when you partake of the Lord's Supper.

REVIEW QUIZ

Use these multiple-choice questions to measure what you learned from this lesson.

1. We are informed that which event in Mark would be told wherever the gospel is proclaimed?
   a. The arrest of Jesus
   b. The Last Supper
   c. Peter's denial of Christ
   d. The woman's anointing of Jesus
2. What book does Jesus quote by saying, "You always have the poor with you" (Mark 14:7)?
   a. Exodus
   b. Leviticus
   c. Numbers
   d. Deuteronomy
3. Some of the disciples were confident that they would not betray Christ.
   a. True
   b. False
4. Which Jewish feast does the Lord's Supper replace?
   a. The Feast of Sabbaths
   b. The Feast of Pentecost
   c. The Feast of Booths
   d. The Feast of Passover
5. Which prophecy foretells Jesus' pouring out His blood for the forgiveness of many?
   a. Jeremiah 31
   b. Jeremiah 32
   c. Isaiah 53
   d. Isaiah 54
6. What does Jesus call the cup after saying, "This is my blood" (Mark 14:24)?
   a. "This blessed wine"
   b. "This blessed cup"
   c. "The fruit of the vine"
   d. "The drink of the vine"

Answer Key—The Night of Jesus' Betrayal

REFLECTION & DISCUSSION QUESTIONS

Before the Video

What Do You Think?

These are personal questions. The answers should be based on your own knowledge and experience.

Scripture Reading

- What elements did Jesus use at the Last Supper? What do they represent and communicate?

  Jesus used bread and wine at the Last Supper. They are fundamental to the sacrament of the Lord's Supper, and they represent the body and blood of Christ, which are, like the bread and wine, broken and poured out for our redemption. When we partake of the body and blood of Jesus, we truly partake of and have communion with Him.

During the Video

The Plot against Jesus

- What did the religious leaders resolve to do during Passover? How did they intend to carry out their plan?

  During the Passover, the scribes and chief priests resolved to arrest and kill Jesus (Mark 14:1). But since they did not want to anger the people and feared backlash if they acted openly during the festival, they sought to arrest Him in secret (vv. 1–2).

- Why did Judas betray Jesus? Is understanding why important for our understanding of the Last Supper?

  Although it is tempting to speculate about why Judas betrayed Jesus, Dr. Godfrey rightfully notes that there is no scriptural clarity on the matter. This is not critical for our understanding of the Last Supper; the key issue to reflect on is whether one is faithful to Christ. The shocking nature of the betrayal itself ought to call us to greater faithfulness to Him.

The Last Supper

- Where did Jesus tell His disciples to go for the Passover meal? What does this command show?

  For the Passover meal, Jesus instructed His disciples to follow a man with a jar into the house, and just as the disciples had had a colt handed over to them merely by stating the Lord's need for it, the man directed them to a room furnished and ready for them to prepare the meal (Mark 14:13–15). Jesus' command is intentionally specific, so that it might clearly show Jesus' prophetic office.

- For whom did Jesus shed His blood, and why is this important?

  As Mark says in the passage, Jesus' blood "is poured out for many" (14:24), which shows that His blood is for only a particular group, the elect, and not for everyone. As the Canons of Dort say, "It is of infinite value and worth" (2.3), but it is given and applied only to those chosen by God (Rom. 8:29–30).

After the Video

- How does the woman's ointment relate to the death of Christ? Why is this important?

  The woman's anointing of Jesus has an important relationship to His death and burial. Just as a person was ordinarily anointed before burial to preserve the body and honor the person, so too was Christ anointed by the woman in anticipation of His atoning sacrifice. This is of great significance, since it shows both the woman's devotion to Jesus and also the importance of honoring Jesus.

- Compare and contrast Judas and Peter. What is the crucial difference between them?

  Both Judas and Peter faltered in their loyalty to Christ—Judas through betrayal and Peter through denial. The critical distinction lies in their responses: Judas displayed worldly sorrow without true repentance, leading to despair, while Peter repented sincerely, leading to restoration (Mark 14:72). In 2 Corinthians 7:10, Paul writes, "For godly grief produces a repentance that leads to salvation without regret, whereas worldly grief produces death."

- What are the four main perspectives on the Lord's Supper? Briefly explain each.

  In the lecture, Dr. Godfrey explained four main views on the Lord's Supper and the meaning of the words of institution (Mark 14:22–24). The first is the Roman Catholic view, which holds that the bread and wine become the body and blood of Christ but still retain the appearance and quality of bread and wine, also known as transubstantiation. *The second is the Lutheran view that the body and blood are ministered to the people in, with, and under the bread and wine, which is commonly known as* consubstantiation. *The third is the Zwinglian view that the supper offers a symbolic partaking of Christ, that it is primarily a memorial of what Christ has done. The final view is the Calvinist view, which holds that through faith, there is a real spiritual feeding on Christ in the supper.*

REVIEW QUIZ

1. **D.**
   Although each of these events is integral to the gospel narrative, the woman who anointed Jesus did such a great and noble deed that Jesus said it would be perpetually remembered (Mark 14:9).

2. **D.**
   When Jesus says, "You always have the poor with you," He is quoting from Deuteronomy 15:11. This chapter emphasizes both the presence of poverty and the Israelites' responsibility to care for the poor (Deut. 15:4, 11).

3. **B.**
   Although most of the disciples wanted to be faithful to Christ, none had a complete assurance of faith. This is why they all asked Jesus, "Is it I?" (Mark 14:19).

4. **D.**
   The Lord's Supper replaces the Jewish Feast of Passover, which is part of why the Lord's Supper is instituted during Passover. Similarly, Paul calls Christ "our Passover lamb" (1 Cor. 5:7); Jesus is the fulfillment of the Passover.

5. **C.**
   The prophecy in Isaiah 53 foretells Jesus' pouring out His blood for the forgiveness of many. Isaiah writes, "Out of the anguish of his soul he shall see and be satisfied; by his knowledge shall the righteous one, my servant, make many to be accounted righteous, and he shall bear their iniquities" (v. 11).

6. **C.**
   After the words of institution, Jesus calls the cup the "fruit of the vine" (Mark 14:25). Dr. Godfrey noted that this goes against the literalist interpretation of the Roman Catholic Church, since Jesus does not strictly speak of the wine as His blood.

23

Deserted by the Disciples

INTRODUCTION

After His final meal, Jesus prepared Himself for the coming betrayal and suffering that He would endure. Though truly divine, He experienced the weight of the cross in His humanity throughout these final hours. In this lesson, Dr. Godfrey covers Christ's betrayal and anguish in the garden of Gethsemane.

LEARNING GOALS

When you have finished this lesson, you should be able to:

- Understand the relationship between Jesus' divinity and humanity during His agony in the garden of Gethsemane
- Explain the theological significance behind Jesus' prayer in the garden
- Identify how Mark uses irony in his description of Jesus' trial

KEY IDEAS

- Jesus was fully aware of His impending betrayal but also the role that its aftermath would play in fulfilling the redemption of His people.
- In His time of suffering, the disciples abandon Christ.
- Jesus is revealed as the truly innocent Lamb of God, willingly offering Himself as a sacrifice for the sins of God's people.

REFLECTION & DISCUSSION QUESTIONS

Before the Video

What Do You Think?

Take a moment to answer the following questions. They will prepare you for the lecture.

- How might knowing that Jesus experienced deep emotional distress shape the way you see Him as a merciful Savior?

- Why didn't any of the disciples stay with Jesus at His arrest? What does Jesus' abandonment show?

Scripture Reading

And Jesus said to them, "Have you come out as against a robber, with swords and clubs to capture me? Day after day I was with you in the temple teaching, and you did not seize me. But let the Scriptures be fulfilled."

—Mark 14:48–9

- Why didn't Jesus stop His arrest?

During the Video

Answer the following questions while you watch the video. They will guide you through the lecture.

Prayer in Gethsemane *0:00–10:29*

- What does Mark mean when he says that Jesus sang a "hymn" (Mark 14:26)?

- What prophetic declaration does Christ make on the Mount of Olives concerning His disciples, and how do they react?

- How can Jesus' prayer be a model for our prayers?

The Betrayal and Arrest of Christ *10:29–23:50*

- How did Jesus react to His betrayal and arrest? How did His disciples react?

- Was Jesus' arrest and trial just? Provide evidence why or why not.

After the Video

Answer the following questions after you have finished the lecture. They will help you identify and summarize the major points.

- Why was Jesus "greatly distressed and troubled" (Mark 14:33)? Does this disprove His divinity? Why or why not?

  If you are in a group, have the members provide an example of Jesus' showing human emotion during His earthly ministry. Ask: How does this relate to His divinity?
- How might the young man who fled hint at Christ's burial and resurrection? What evidence supports this idea?

  If you are in a group, have the members share what they think of Dr. Godfrey's theory about the young man. Ask: Do you consider it convincing or not?
- How is Jesus' trial filled with irony? What testifies to its irony?

  If you are in a group, have the members point out earlier uses of irony in Mark's gospel. What do these instances of irony show us about Jesus?

PRAYER

Commit what you have learned from God's Word in this lesson to prayer.

- Praise God that nothing is outside of His control or can take Him by surprise.
- Confess the times that you, like the disciples, seem to flee from Christ in moments of temptation or trial.
- Thank God for Jesus' faithfulness, even in the face of betrayal and suffering.
- Ask God to strengthen your faith and courage as a witness to Christ.

REVIEW QUIZ

Use these multiple-choice questions to measure what you learned from this lesson.

1. What psalms were traditionally sung at Passover?
   a. Psalms 113–118
   b. Psalms 113–119
   c. Psalms 116–119
   d. Psalms 120–134
2. What earlier event in Mark does Peter's denial mirror and complete?
   a. The transfiguration
   b. The triumphal entry
   c. The questioning of Christ
   d. The Last Supper
3. Which quotation of Psalm 75 does Jesus employ in His prayer to the Father?
   a. "At the set time that I appoint I will judge with equity."
   b. "But I will declare it forever; I will sing praises to the God of Jacob."
   c. "It is God who executes judgment, putting down one and lifting up another."
   d. "In the hand of the Lord there is a cup with foaming wine, well mixed."
4. Which disciple was at the foot of the cross during the crucifixion?
   a. Peter
   b. James
   c. John
   d. None of the above
5. We know that the young man who fled from the Romans was Mark.
   a. True
   b. False
6. Which psalm did Dr. Godfrey connect with the failed testimony of Jesus' enemies?
   a. Psalm 1
   b. Psalm 2
   c. Psalm 3
   d. Psalm 4

Answer Key—Deserted by the Disciples

REFLECTION & DISCUSSION QUESTIONS

Before the Video

What Do You Think?

These are personal questions. The answers should be based on your own knowledge and experience.

Scripture Reading

- Why didn't Jesus stop His arrest?

  Jesus did not stop His arrest because He knew that it was necessary not only for the salvation of God's people but also that the Scriptures might be fulfilled. He did this to further show that He is the true Prophet and fulfillment of prophecy.

During the Video

Prayer in Gethsemane

- What does Mark mean when he says that Jesus sang a "hymn" (Mark 14:26)?

  When Mark states that Jesus and the disciples sang a hymn, he is most likely referring to their singing a psalm, since that was the Jewish custom after the Passover meal. This is notable because it shows that Scripture does not always use the word that we might be accustomed to, just as Paul uses the word "psalm" to refer to a hymn (1 Cor. 14:26).

- What prophetic declaration does Christ make on the Mount of Olives concerning His disciples, and how do they react?

  Jesus quotes Zechariah 13:7, emphasizing that He, as the Shepherd, will be struck and His disciples will scatter (Mark 14:27). His disciples promise to never deny Him, but they also miss the fact that these things will give way to Jesus' future resurrection and glorification (v. 28).

- How can Jesus' prayer be a model for our prayers?

  Jesus' prayer at Gethsemane is, in many ways, a model prayer for us because it reveals that we can express our deepest feelings to God. We also are always to submit our prayers to the will of God, whatever our desire may be. For this reason, everyone should pray, "Yet not what I will, but what you will" (Mark 14:36).

The Betrayal and Arrest of Christ

- How did Jesus react to His betrayal and arrest? How did His disciples react?

  Jesus was not surprised by Judas' betrayal and knew that He would be handed over to wicked men, that "the Scriptures [would] be fulfilled" (Mark 14:49). The disciples, on the other hand, all fled. Even Peter, after drawing and using a sword to defend Jesus (John 18:3–11), would abandon Him. This is the last time the disciples appear in Jesus' presence in Mark's gospel.

- Was Jesus' arrest and trial just? Provide evidence why or why not.

  Jesus was unjustly arrested and tried for a capital offense. This can be demonstrated from the false testimony that various witnesses gave against Him, since they could not agree on their testimony (Mark 14:59). Furthermore, even if they had provided a unified testimony against Him, this could not have lawfully convicted Jesus and warranted the death sentence.

After the Video

- Why was Jesus "greatly distressed and troubled" (Mark 14:33)? Does this disprove His divinity? Why or why not?

  Jesus was "greatly distressed and troubled" because He was about to endure the greatest suffering that has ever been suffered. Although the expression of these human emotions may seem contrary to His divinity, it is necessary to remember that Jesus was both truly God and truly man. As the Son of God, He took on true flesh (John 1:14) and He truly expressed the full range of human emotions, yet without sin (Heb. 4:15). As Dr. Godfrey stated, "There is a tendency in our theology to allow the divinity of Jesus to swallow up the humanity," so we must be careful to uphold one without compromising the other.

- How might the young man who fled hint at Christ's burial and resurrection? What evidence supports this idea?

  The flight of the young man, a detail that is unique to Mark's gospel (Mark 14:51–52), may hint at the coming resurrection of Christ for a few reasons. First, the linen cloth is left behind while the young man flees, and the word for "linen cloth" is the same word used to describe the shroud in which Jesus is buried. Second, the only other use of this word for "young man" in Mark's gospel is for the one who is in the empty tomb in Mark 16 when the women come on Easter morning (v. 5). These are the subtle echoes of death and resurrection in this moment in Mark 14.

- How is Jesus' trial filled with irony? What testifies to its irony?

  Jesus' trial is filled with irony because of the contrast between the false accusations and Jesus' identity as the Son of God and the perfection of His character. A good example of this is how the chief priests, after finding no consistent witness against Christ, ask Him to testify against Himself (Mark 14:60). While Jesus appears to be guilty by His silence, in reality, the priests are convicting themselves by their own testimony. The entirety of the trial self-attests to the truthfulness of Jesus, and as He continues to be questioned, this only becomes more evident.

REVIEW QUIZ

1. **A.**
   Psalms 113–118 were traditionally sung by Jews during the Passover. This is significant because it gives the proper context for Jesus and His disciples' singing (Mark 14:26) as well as the quotation of Psalm 118 at the triumphal entry (11:9).
2. **C.**
   Mark uses Peter's threefold denial of Christ to echo the three questions asked of Him in Mark 12. Just as Peter answers three questions with a denial of Christ, so too is Jesus questioned three times by the leaders concerning His own authority.
3. **D.**
   When Jesus prays to the Father in Gethsemane, His reference to the cup of God's wrath alludes to Psalm 75:8. This passage also speaks of the wicked's drinking the cup down to the dregs, which is noteworthy because Jesus is going to drink the cup not for His wickedness but for ours (2 Cor. 5:21).
4. **C.**
   Although Mark does not record any of the Apostles' being at the scene of the crucifixion, John was present, as his gospel records (John 19:26). This is not a contradiction, but Mark does this to highlight the abandonment of Christ on the cross.
5. **B.**
   Although the early church speculated that the young man who fled was Mark, the text provides no certainty of his identity.
6. **B.**
   Dr. Godfrey connected the failed testimony during Jesus' trial with Psalm 2. This is because, in spite of His enemies' accusations, they have no actual ground for accusing Jesus, since even their lies contradict them. For this reason, it is fitting that Psalm 2 says, "The Lord holds them in derision" (v. 4).

24

Jesus' Trial and Peter's Denial

INTRODUCTION

As Jesus faces His final hours before His crucifixion, He undergoes a series of trials before the religious and political authorities of Judea. Meanwhile, Peter is tested and his faith is put through a spiritual trial. In this lesson, Dr. Godfrey continues through Jesus' final night, explaining what the details teach us about Jesus and the lesson we can learn from Peter's denial.

LEARNING GOALS

When you have finished this lesson, you should be able to:

- Describe how Jesus interacted with the high priests during His trial
- Compare and contrast the responses of Jesus and Peter as they were tested
- Explain the character and motives of Pilate as depicted in the Gospels

KEY IDEAS

- Jesus explicitly affirmed His identity as the Messiah and the Son of God.
- Mark intended for Peter's denial to be an instructive example for all believers.
- Pilate's questioning of Jesus is driven by political interests rather than the pursuit of truth.

REFLECTION & DISCUSSION QUESTIONS

Before the Video

What Do You Think?

Take a moment to answer the following questions. They will prepare you for the lecture.

- Why might Jesus have endured false accusations and mockery from His adversaries?
- Is it possible for a true Christian to deny Jesus? Why or why not?

Scripture Reading

And as Peter was below in the courtyard, one of the servant girls of the high priest came, and seeing Peter warming himself, she looked at him and said, "You also were with the Nazarene, Jesus." But he denied it, saying, "I neither know nor understand what you mean." And he went out into the gateway and the rooster crowed. And the servant girl saw him and began again to say to the bystanders, "This man is one of them." But again he denied it. And after a little while the bystanders again said to Peter, "Certainly you are one of them, for you are a Galilean." But he began to invoke a curse on himself and to swear, "I do not know this man of whom you speak." And immediately the rooster crowed a second time. And Peter remembered how Jesus had said to him, "Before the rooster crows twice, you will deny me three times." And he broke down and wept.

—Mark 14:66–72

- What details make Peter's denials so heartbreaking? How did Peter react after denying Christ?

During the Video

Answer the following questions while you watch the video. They will guide you through the lecture.

The Great I Am — *0:00–9:21*

- How does Jesus answer the question, "Are you the Christ, the Son of the Blessed?" (Mark 14:61)? Why does He respond this way?
- Why did Caiaphas accuse Jesus of blasphemy? Did Jesus blaspheme? Explain.

Peter's Denial and Pilate's Questioning *9:21–24:12*

- Why does Peter follow behind Jesus? Why does Mark make note of this?

- When Pilate asks Jesus about His identity, how does He respond? Why is this significant?

After the Video

Answer the following questions after you have finished the lecture. They will help you identify and summarize the major points.

- How does Jesus prophesy during His trial with the priests? How does He respond to their command to prophesy? Why?

  If you are in a group, have the members discuss how Christ's actions under persecution can be imitated daily. Ask: What are some examples of this?

- Compare and contrast the trial of Peter and the trial of Christ. What are some notable similarities and differences?

  If you are in a group, have some of the members give an example of how they have acted like Peter in his lowest moment in the Gospels. Ask: How did you turn to Christ afterward?

- How does Pilate act in the Gospels? How does this affect his disposition and attitude toward Jesus?

  If you are in a group, have the members discuss what Pilate's statements and actions reveal about Jesus. Ask: Why didn't Pilate stop the crucifixion?

PRAYER

Commit what you have learned from God's Word in this lesson to prayer.

- Praise God for His majesty revealed even in moments of darkness.
- Confess the times that you have, like Peter, stumbled in your faith and in commitment to Christ.
- Thank God for sending a Savior who was willing to suffer on your behalf.
- Ask God's Spirit to create in you a steadfast heart and a willingness to imitate Christ under persecution and false accusation.

REVIEW QUIZ

Use these multiple-choice questions to measure what you learned from this lesson.

1. When questioned, how does Jesus reinforce that He is the Messiah?
   a. He reveals His glory to Caiaphas.
   b. He foretells His coming glory to Caiaphas.
   c. He reveals His glory to the centurion.
   d. He gives no sign to prove His status.

2. What part of Mark's trial record is a reference to Isaiah 50?
   a. "They all condemned him as deserving death."
   b. "You have heard his blasphemy."
   c. "Some began to spit on him."
   d. "The guards received him with blows."

3. What event is at the center of Dr. Godfrey's eighth chiasm?
   a. Jesus' crucifixion
   b. Jesus' burial
   c. Peter's denial
   d. The centurion's confession

4. What is a more literal translation of the words "servant girl" (Mark 14:69)?
   a. "Little girl"
   b. "Youth"
   c. "Slave woman"
   d. "Daughter"

5. Mark wants us to understand that stumbling in our faithfulness, as Peter did, is unforgivable.
   a. True
   b. False

6. What time of day did the chief priests deliver Jesus over to Pilate?
   a. Night
   b. Evening
   c. Afternoon
   d. Morning

Answer Key—Jesus' Trial and Peter's Denial

REFLECTION & DISCUSSION QUESTIONS

Before the Video

What Do You Think?

These are personal questions. The answers should be based on your own knowledge and experience.

Scripture Reading

- What details make Peter's denials so heartbreaking? How did Peter react after denying Christ?

  Peter's denial was emphatic, but his denial was also in answer to the questioning of a servant girl. Peter had been so confident that he would not deny Christ, but at the moment of testing he did not even embrace his identity as a Christian before a servant girl. After denying Christ, Peter immediately wept out of sorrow for his faithlessness. He did this because he remembered what Jesus had said about him and, recognizing that Jesus' prophecy was true of him, lamented his sin.

During the Video

The Great I Am

- How does Jesus answer the question, "Are you the Christ, the Son of the Blessed?" (Mark 14:61)? Why does He respond this way?

  When the high priest asks Jesus whether He is the Christ and Son of God, He concisely responds, "I am" (Mark 14:62), which evokes the divine name but also fully affirms His identity as the Christ. Through most of Mark's gospel, Jesus has been avoiding an explicit answer to this question. Christ answers so directly because His hour has finally come, bearing witness to the truth while under trial.

- Why did Caiaphas accuse Jesus of blasphemy? Did Jesus blaspheme? Explain.

  The only reason that Caiaphas called Jesus a blasphemer is that he did not believe that Jesus was actually who He said He was (Mark 14:63–64). For Jesus, claiming to be the Christ was not blasphemy because it proclaimed the truth of His identity.

Peter's Denial and Pilate's Questioning

- Why does Peter follow behind Jesus? Why does Mark make note of this?

  Peter seems to follow behind Jesus because he still believes that he is going to be the faithful and committed follower. Dr. Godfrey takes this paradigm as a pattern for Christians; he says, "I think Mark intends this to be, in a profound sense, a way of thinking about ourselves." The model of Peter serves to ask believers whether they have truly understood the call to faith.

- When Pilate asks Jesus about His identity, how does He respond? Why is this significant?

  When Pilate asks Jesus whether He is "the King of the Jews," Jesus responds by saying, "You have said so" (Mark 15:2). Dr. Godfrey notes that this has the same meaning as the English phrase "so they say." Therefore, Jesus is not answering the question one way or the other; instead, He carefully gives an answer that does not align Him with false messianic expectations or Pilate's political understanding of His identity.

After the Video

- How does Jesus prophesy during His trial with the priests? How does He respond to their command to prophesy? Why?

  Jesus prophesies during His trial with the priests by telling Caiaphas the high priest of His future glory and ascension. Yet even after He does this, the other priests still command Him to prophesy to prove His identity as the Messiah. Instead of prophesying, as Jesus had done throughout His whole ministry, He stays silent and thus condemns these men to a famine of God's Word. He does this because the religious leaders already have hard hearts and fail to heed His prophecy, but also to give the judgment of Amos 8, which proclaims a famine "of hearing the words of the Lord" (v. 11).

- Compare and contrast the trial of Peter and the trial of Christ. What are some notable similarities and differences?

  Dr. Godfrey noted that Peter and Jesus both went through a type of trial. Jesus was questioned and ridiculed, yet He did not fail when tested and tried by the chief priests. On the other hand, Peter was tried and tested by a lowly servant girl, yet he denied Christ multiple times. They were both men of God who had their faith tested, but only one of them was proved right and true: the true and faithful Jesus Christ.

- How does Pilate act in the Gospels? How does this affect his disposition and attitude toward Jesus?

  Pilate is portrayed as politically motivated, indifferent to the substance of the controversy surrounding Jesus. This is why Pilate is merely concerned with whether Jesus is "the King of the Jews" (Mark 15:2) and not whether Jesus is a heretic, blasphemer, or religious extremist. He seeks to avoid conflict with the Jewish leaders or to defy the crowd after they are stirred up to release Barabbas. He prioritizes political stability over justice, which ultimately leads to Jesus' condemnation despite Pilate's recognizing Jesus' innocence.

REVIEW QUIZ

1. **B.**
   Jesus proves His claim to be the Messiah by foretelling His coming glory to Caiaphas the high priest. Not only does He prophesy of His glory, but Jesus also tells Caiaphas that He will directly reveal it to him by stating, "You will see the Son of Man seated at the right hand of Power, and coming with the clouds of heaven" (Mark 14:62).

2. **C.**
   Mark's trial record references Isaiah 50 when it reads, "Some began to spit on him" (Mark 14:65). This is because Isaiah had prophesied, "I hid not my face from disgrace and spitting" (Isa. 50:6).

3. **C.**
   Dr. Godfrey's eighth chiasm is centered on Peter's denial. While this is not meant to undermine the importance of Christ's death and burial, it does put an emphasis on Peter's actions and further emphasizes Mark's call to faith.

4. **A.**
   A more literal translation of the word for "servant girl" would be "little girl." This is noteworthy, since such a person would have been of little esteem, and yet Peter cowers before her.

5. **B.**
   The message of the gospel is that even the worst of sins can be forgiven if you repent, if you turn to Christ for mercy, and this is later seen in Peter's restoration.

6. **D.**
   The chief priests delivered Jesus over to Pilate in the morning after they held a council (Mark 15:1).

25

Why Have You Forsaken Me?

INTRODUCTION

Jesus underwent a crucifixion of profound humiliation and suffering. In this lesson, Dr. Godfrey explains the theological significance of Christ's death, highlighting how He fulfills the ultimate purpose of His earthly ministry: to redeem God's people through His forsakenness on the cross.

LEARNING GOALS

When you have finished this lesson, you should be able to:

- Understand why Jesus suffered in the specific ways that He did
- Identify key Old Testament references and fulfillments during the crucifixion
- Explain the significance of Jesus' forsakenness on the cross

KEY IDEAS

- Jesus was treated like a defeated king by the Romans.
- Salvation is accomplished through the mighty power of humble suffering.
- Mark highlights the fulfillment of Scripture in Christ's crucifixion.

REFLECTION & DISCUSSION QUESTIONS

Before the Video

What Do You Think?

Take a moment to answer the following questions. They will prepare you for the lecture.

- Why is it ironic that Jesus was mocked as "King of the Jews" (Mark 15:2)?
- Why was it necessary for Christ to die?

Scripture Reading

And when the sixth hour had come, there was darkness over the whole land until the ninth hour. And at the ninth hour Jesus cried with a loud voice, "Eloi, Eloi, lema sabachthani?" which means, "My God, my God, why have you forsaken me?"

—Mark 15:33–34

- What sign occurred during the last hours of Jesus' life? What does this passage suggest that it signified?

During the Video

Answer the following questions while you watch the video. They will guide you through the lecture.

Christ Crucified *0:00–12:08*

- What did the soldiers do to Jesus? Why did they do these things?
- How painful was carrying the cross for Jesus? Did He try to stop the pain?
- What did the bystanders at the cross think a savior was? What about Mark?

Christ Abandoned *12:08–23:32*

- What significant promise did God make to His people in the Old Testament? What does this mean for the cross?

- Who stayed with Jesus throughout His life and death? How did they do so?

After the Video

Answer the following questions after you have finished the lecture. They will help you identify and summarize the major points.

- Explain the relationship between Psalm 22 and the crucifixion. What are some relevant verses in that psalm?

  If you are in a group, have a few members read some of the messianic psalms—such as Psalms 2, 8, 16, 91, 110—and explain how each one applies to Christ.

- How is the tearing of the curtain important? What does it mean for believers?

  If you are in a group, have the members discuss why it is significant that Christ fulfilled the old covenant. Ask: How should we relate now to the old covenant institutions that Christ fulfilled?

- How do Isaiah's prophecies relate to the forsakenness of Christ on the cross? Give Scripture references.

  If you are in a group, have the members discuss how the forsakenness of Christ challenges them to greater obedience. Ask: What should we do if we are forsaken by the world on account of Christ?

PRAYER

Commit what you have learned from God's Word in this lesson to prayer.

- Praise God for the perfection of our suffering King.
- Confess the ways that you fail to live in gratitude for Christ's sacrifice.
- Thank God for your forgiveness through Christ's forsakenness.
- Ask God to give you humility to consider others as greater than yourself (see Phil. 2:1–11).

REVIEW QUIZ

Use these multiple-choice questions to measure what you learned from this lesson.

1. In the Roman Empire, when were kings ordinarily led in a procession unto crucifixion?
   a. When they blasphemed the gods
   b. When they failed to pay tribute
   c. When they were conquered by Caesar
   d. After they failed as Caesar
2. Crucifixion was essentially death by what?
   a. Blood loss
   b. Asphyxiation
   c. Thirst
   d. All of the above
3. What Old Testament prophet prophesies of the darkness at Jesus' death?
   a. Amos
   b. Joel
   c. Hosea
   d. Habakkuk
4. Who identified Jesus as the Son of God on the cross?
   a. Pilate
   b. The centurion
   c. The military tribune
   d. The Roman prefect
5. Crucifixion victims were not usually given a burial.
   a. True
   b. False
6. What action of Christ fulfills the Sabbath?
   a. His crucifixion
   b. His trial
   c. His teaching
   d. His burial

Answer Key—Why Have You Forsaken Me?

REFLECTION & DISCUSSION QUESTIONS

Before the Video

What Do You Think?

These are personal questions. The answers should be based on your own knowledge and experience.

Scripture Reading

- What sign occurred during the last hours of Jesus' life? What does this passage suggest that it signified?

  When Jesus was in His final moments, the whole land went dark. This occurred to highlight the forsakenness of Christ on the cross and show, to a greater degree, the magnitude of the suffering that took place in His death and the significance of the God-man's dying on the cross.

During the Video

Christ Crucified

- What did the soldiers do to Jesus? Why did they do these things?

  After Pilate released Barabbas to the crowd, Jesus was handed over to Roman soldiers. They scourged Him with whips embedded with bone fragments, mocked Him by clothing Him in a purple cloak, and crowned Him with thorns. These actions were meant to humiliate Him and to parody His claim to kingship. Dr. Godfrey suggests that they did this because they had likely overheard the conversation with Pilate.

- How painful was carrying the cross for Jesus? Did He try to stop the pain?

  Jesus was in so much pain when He took up the cross that another man, Simon of Cyrene, had to carry it for Him to Golgotha (Mark 15:21; Luke 23:26). In spite of all the pain that He was enduring, however, Jesus refused to take myrrh and wine to soothe Himself because He had resolved to take the full cup of God's wrath for the sake of His people (see Mark 14:36).

- What did the bystanders at the cross think a savior was? What about Mark?

  The bystanders at the cross thought a savior was someone who could demonstrate his power—in this case, by saving himself from the cross. In contrast, Mark shows that the true Savior is the One who endures all for His people (Isa. 53:11), which is why Dr. Godfrey says that "only a helpless Savior can save."

Christ Abandoned

- What significant promise did God make to His people in the Old Testament? What does this mean for the cross?

  In the Old Testament, God promised His people that He would "not leave you or forsake you" (Deut. 31:6). This applies to Jesus on the cross by revealing that He will not truly be forsaken forever, but instead He will be raised from His state of forsakenness and be vindicated in the Holy Spirit (1 Tim. 3:16).

- Who stayed with Jesus throughout His life and death? How did they do so?

  Despite Jesus' abandonment on the cross, Mark notes that the women who followed Him remained with Christ even to His death (Mark 15:40–41, 47), and they were the first to witness His resurrection (16:1).

After the Video

- Explain the relationship between Psalm 22 and the crucifixion. What are some relevant verses in that psalm?

  Psalm 22 is a prophecy that, although originally spoken by David, describes Jesus' crucifixion. Verse 18 says, "They divide my garments among them, and for my clothing they cast lots," which foretells the lots that soldiers would cast for Jesus' garments (Mark 15:24). At a more climactic moment, Jesus quotes Psalm 22:1 before dying when He says, "My God, my God, why have you forsaken me?" (Mark 15:34). These weighty prophecies both attest to the authenticity of Jesus' claims and establish the authority and importance of the Old Testament.

- How is the tearing of the curtain important? What does it mean for believers?

  In the lecture, Dr. Godfrey recorded multiple pivotal ideas that are summed up in the tearing of the curtain (Mark 15:38). First, it is the only other place that the word "torn" is used in Mark's gospel, marking the end of Jesus' ministry, as contrasted with the beginning and the tearing of the heavens at His baptism (1:10). Second, it shows that the death of Christ is an act of God, since the curtain was torn from top to bottom, which no man could have done because of its size. Finally, this event declares that Jesus is the true temple and that believers are all united in His priesthood and temple.

- How do Isaiah's prophecies relate to the forsakenness of Christ on the cross? Give Scripture references.

  Isaiah's prophecies, particularly in the latter half of the book (chs. 40–66), have much to say about Jesus, even in regard to His forsakenness on the cross. For example, Isaiah writes, "For a brief moment I deserted you, but with great compassion I will gather you" (Isa. 54:7), which shows that despite Christ's being forsaken on the cross, He will be gathered (or raised up) again after the cross. Furthermore, Isaiah notes that God is a strong and mighty leader, for He does not forsake His works (42:16), just as Jesus would be raised from the dead.

REVIEW QUIZ

1. **C.**
   In the Roman Empire, defeated kings were often led in a humiliating procession and then crucified to display their total subjugation to Caesar. Jesus was subjected to similar treatment, mocked with the crown of thorns and purple cloak and derided as "King of the Jews."

2. **B.**
   The practice of crucifixion involved death by asphyxiation, or lack of oxygen to the body. This was because the pain and injuries sustained before crucifixion would cause the victim to eventually lose the strength to breathe.

3. **A.**
   The Old Testament prophet Amos prophesies of a time when the Lord "will make the sun go down at noon and darken the earth in broad daylight" (Amos 8:9). This is exactly in line with the darkness accompanying the death of Christ as a sign of judgment over Judea (Mark 15:33).

4. **B.**
   When Jesus breathed His last on the cross, the centurion who was standing there recognized Him as the Son of God (Mark 15:39). The uniqueness of Jesus' death made such an impression on the man that he could come to no other conclusion.

5. **A.**
   Although Jesus was given a burial by Joseph of Arimathea (Mark 15:45–46), this was not a typical practice in the Roman Empire. On the contrary, crucified people were treated as traitors and were not given an honorable burial.

6. **D.**
   The burial of Christ fulfills the Jewish Sabbath, since it is the end of the old creation and its corresponding rest. In place of this, His resurrection constitutes the Lord's Day, or Christian Sabbath, of the new creation that He begins (Rev. 1:10).

26

Meeting the Risen Christ

INTRODUCTION

Jesus' resurrection marks the triumphant conclusion to the gospel of Mark. But why did Mark present the good news of the resurrection so abruptly? And where does the gospel of Mark really end? In this final lesson, Dr. Godfrey examines the ending of Mark's gospel, offering insights into the manuscript evidence and stylistic elements of Mark's longer ending and theological implications of Mark 16:1–8.

LEARNING GOALS

When you have finished this lesson, you should be able to:

- Explain the major perspectives on the ending of Mark's gospel
- Understand the importance of Galilee in Mark's gospel
- Identify the message and themes present in the ending of Mark

KEY IDEAS

- There is conflicting manuscript data concerning where Mark's gospel ends.
- Galilee symbolizes a return to the beginning of Jesus' ministry and a renewed understanding of His work.
- The abrupt ending of Mark is intentional, confronting readers with the reality of the resurrection and our need to proclaim it.

REFLECTION & DISCUSSION QUESTIONS

Before the Video

What Do You Think?

Take a moment to answer the following questions. They will prepare you for the lecture.

- Why did God allow the Bible to have different manuscript witnesses? How can this be helpful? How might it be difficult?

- Why is Mark such a short gospel? How does his ending reflect the rest of his gospel?

Scripture Reading

And he said to them, "Do not be alarmed. You seek Jesus of Nazareth, who was crucified. He has risen; he is not here. See the place where they laid him. But go, tell his disciples and Peter that he is going before you to Galilee. There you will see him, just as he told you."

—Mark 16:6–7

- Why does the angel say "just as he told you" (Mark 16:7)? What had Jesus told the disciples?

During the Video

Answer the following questions while you watch the video. They will guide you through the lecture.

Which Ending? *0:00–9:55*

- What is the only unique thing in the longer ending of Mark?

- What stylistic elements of Mark give evidence for the short ending?

The Resurrection *9:55–23:49*

- Did the women expect the resurrection? Why or why not?

- How do angels typically greet people? Why?

- Why is it significant that Peter is named in the angel's message?

After the Video

Answer the following questions after you have finished the lecture. They will help you identify and summarize the major points.

- What are three major views about the ending of Mark's gospel? Briefly explain each.

  If you are in a group, have the members discuss whether they are inclined toward one view or another and why.

- Why does the angel tell the women to go to Galilee? What does this return to Galilee mean for the disciples?

  If you are in a group, have the members reflect on the disciples' return to Galilee. Ask: If you could begin your walk with Christ anew, what would be different?

- What is "the 'Oh, No' Effect"? Why is it important for Mark's ending?

  If you are in a group, have the members explain their impressions of Mark's abrupt ending. Ask: How does it compare to the other gospels?

PRAYER

Commit what you have learned from God's Word in this lesson to prayer.

- Praise God for the wonderful and sure hope of the resurrection.
- Confess any times that you have kept your mouth closed in fear rather than opening it in joy of the resurrection.
- Thank God for the disciples' witness of the resurrection of Christ.
- Ask God to help you walk in the Spirit with the resurrected Christ, since you have been raised with Him so that you may put sin to death.

REVIEW QUIZ

Use these multiple-choice questions to measure what you learned from this lesson.

1. Most early manuscripts include the longer ending to Mark's gospel.
   a. True
   b. False
2. What type of document best characterizes the gospel of Mark?
   a. Apologetic
   b. Evangelistic
   c. Historical
   d. Ecclesial
3. What unique term from Mark 14 is repeated in chapter 16?
   a. "Young man"
   b. "Nazareth"
   c. "The first day of the week"
   d. "A white robe"
4. Who thought that Jesus' body might have been taken away?
   a. Mary, the mother of Jesus
   b. Mary Magdalene
   c. Salome
   d. Peter and John
5. Which particular disciple did the angel tell the women to speak to?
   a. James the Greater
   b. James the Lesser
   c. Peter
   d. John
6. Which of the following is *not* a view about the ending of Mark?
   a. It ends at verse 8.
   b. The original ending was lost.
   c. The long ending was written by Luke.
   d. The long ending is authentic.

Answer Key—Meeting the Risen Christ

REFLECTION & DISCUSSION QUESTIONS

Before the Video

What Do You Think?

These are personal questions. The answers should be based on your own knowledge and experience.

Scripture Reading

- Why does the angel say "just as he told you" (Mark 16:7)? What had Jesus told the disciples?

  The angel at the tomb says "just as he told you" because Jesus had prophesied about His death and resurrection to the disciples earlier. In chapter 8, Mark writes, "He began to teach them that the Son of Man must suffer many things and be rejected by the elders and the chief priests and the scribes and be killed, and after three days rise again" (Mark 8:31).

During the Video

Which Ending?

- What is the only unique thing in the longer ending of Mark?

  Compared to the end of the other gospels, the only unique claim Mark makes is found in 16:18 and deals with the handling of snakes and the drinking of poison. The rest of the ending is largely similar to material in other gospels.

- What stylistic elements of Mark give evidence for the short ending?

  One of the ways that Dr. Godfrey argues for the shorter ending of Mark is by marshaling the book's overall style. Mark tends to speak abruptly with terms such as "immediately," but this sense of urgency and immediacy is not present in the longer ending. The change in style that is present in the longer ending provides a significant argument for the shorter ending.

The Resurrection

- Did the women expect the resurrection? Why or why not?

  The women did not expect the resurrection. They brought burial spices to anoint Jesus' body and were worrying about who would roll the stone away from the tomb (Mark 16:1, 3). These actions reveal that they assumed that Jesus remained dead in the tomb and that He had not risen.

- How do angels typically greet people? Why?

  When angels appear to people, they typically greet them with the words "Fear not" or, in Mark's case, "Do not be alarmed" (Mark 16:6). This is because angels are alarming in their glory and power, such as the seraphim in Isaiah 6:2. Angels do not look like babies or other harmless-appearing creatures, as popularly characterized; instead, they magnificently display the glory of God.

- Why is it significant that Peter is named in the angel's message?

  When the angel commands the women to tell the disciples about the resurrection, he singles out Peter in particular (Mark 16:7). Dr. Godfrey notes that this is probably because even though Peter utterly failed to be faithful, Christ still wants to meet with him.

After the Video

- What are three major views about the ending of Mark's gospel? Briefly explain each.

  Because of debate concerning the manuscript and internal evidence for the longer ending of Mark, scholars tend to take one of three views to deal with the evidence. First, some people hold that the entire long ending (Mark 16:9–20) is authentic to the original text of Mark. Others agree that there is a longer ending but propose that it was lost early on. Finally, some say that the legitimate ending is verse 8, and that Mark intended for it to be abrupt.

- Why does the angel tell the women to go to Galilee? What does this return to Galilee mean for the disciples?

  The angel tells the women to meet Jesus in Galilee because that is where He began His public ministry. This means that the disciples are invited to, in a sense, relive and fully understand the ministry of Jesus. They are going to meet Jesus, not with hardened hearts (Mark 6:52), but now with eyes open through the light of the resurrection. This is not some new revelation, but it is in accordance with Jesus' plan from the beginning (8:31; 9:30–32; 10:32–34).

- What is "the 'Oh, No' Effect"? Why is it important for Mark's ending?

  "The 'Oh, No' Effect" is the term that Dr. Godfrey used to describe the very last verse of Mark, which states that the women "said nothing to anyone, for they were afraid" (v. 8). This ending is so abrupt and counterintuitive that it may frighten the reader, but Dr. Godfrey perceived that Mark knows that this will not be the last word, but that the women will eventually speak—and perhaps it is a call to his readers that this is the good news that they must proclaim. The resurrection is simply too glorious for the news not to spread, which is why the other gospels do show the women speaking and all of Jesus' disciples coming to a knowledge of His victory.

REVIEW QUIZ

1. **B.**
   Although some manuscripts do contain Mark 16:9–20, the majority of early manuscripts end at verse 8. This is important, since the earlier manuscripts are likely to be more authentic than the later ones.

2. **D.**
   Dr. Godfrey said that the gospel of Mark is not an apologetic document and is not meant for unbelievers. This is not to dismiss evangelistic or historical qualities, but it shows that Mark was written with an ecclesial goal in mind, since it is for the believers in the church.

3. **A.**
   The use of "young man" in Mark 14:51–52 is repeated in 16:5, and these are the only two uses of the term in Mark's gospel. As Dr. Godfrey noted earlier in the series, the themes of death and resurrection and angelic motifs might be present in Mark 14 because of this.

4. **B.**
   In John's gospel, Mary Magdalene originally thought that Jesus' body had been taken away and put elsewhere before Jesus revealed Himself to her (John 20:13). This helps explain the fear and trembling that the women experienced upon hearing the angel's proclamation in addition to their alarm at seeing the angel himself.

5. **C.**
   When the angel commanded the women to tell the disciples about the resurrection, he singled out Peter in particular (Mark 16:7), which shows the care of our Lord in assuring Peter that He wanted to meet with him despite his denial of Him.

6. **C.**
   The idea that the long ending of Mark was written by Luke is not a recognized scholarly view. The three main perspectives on Mark's ending are that (1) it concludes at verse 8, (2) the original ending was lost, and (3) the long ending is authentic but was added later.